MW01242790

ONE PILOT'S MEMOIR

NEVER FLEW JETS...

RICHARD HERRMANN

Second Edition

Copyright © 2019 by Hold That Thought Publishing Company
Bellingham, Washington

All rights reserved.

No portion of this book may be reproduced or utilized in any form,
or by any electronic, mechanical, or other means,
without the prior written permission of the publisher.

Additional copies of **NEVER FLEW JETS...**
may be ordered from Amazon.com

COVER PHOTO: Thank you celebration by local natives for a food lift to Silimo, Irian Papua, Indonesia during the drought and famine in June of 1998.

Disclaimer: To my recollection, the events depicted here are accurate. However, should I be questioned by the FAA, CIA, FBI or local police, in order to protect myself from fines, loss of license or imprisonment, I may have to claim dementia, old age or a pilot's propensity to embellish – occasionally.

Daughter Liana likes this plane!

IN MEMORY

of those special aviating friends who had suddenly gone West, into the sunset, without being able to tell their stories.

Fred (Alaska)
Bob Rick
Tim Wilkerson
Dave Weinberger
Paul Davis
Paul Mitchell
Ron Workman
Dave Rahm
Dan Weber
Jose Ferraz
Frank Babcock
John Galen
Verdie Erickson
Jorge (Honduras)
Bruce Heiner
Jim Crawley
Sparky Imeson

Looking forward to meeting you guys again, somewhere, at a big table in the corner for some more hangar flying.

ACKNOWLEDGEMENTS

I think man has always wanted to fly, and why not? Look at the birds soaring above our beautiful earth, over rivers, seas and mountains. How could one not be envious? The mythological Greek, Daedalus, warned his son about the dangers of flying too close to the sun but Icarus was too enraptured by flight to pay attention and melted the wax holding the feathers to his wings and crashed. Dreamers like Leonardo da Vinci could have been called our first aeronautical engineers, but their ideas preceded the technology of that era. Gliders and balloons finally put man into the air, but with limitations until the Wright brothers came along and built and flew the first heavier than air flying machines. Finally, the engineers, aerodynamicists, builders and mechanics of the last 116 years who made the safe, beautiful and easy flying, as we know it today, available to all of us. To them, I am eternally grateful.

To the flight instructors who turned my dream into reality and those employers who trusted me with their planes and passengers which turned my passion into a livelihood, I thank you.

Mostly, I want to thank my family for allowing me to chase my dreams. My loving wife, Rica, and our two daughters, Christy and Liana, spent many days and nights without a husband or dad. Thank you so much for tolerating my passion.

Finally, I want to thank my friend Jerry Johnson for helping me put my thoughts onto these pages and my many friends who encouraged me and proofread my drafts. Unfortunately, some mistakes still slipped through grammar and spell check and I wish to thank the readers of the first edition for finding those errors and forwarding them to me. This has also given me the opportunity to add a few passages which I hope are relevant and interesting.

Charles Mutugi Kiara, a teenage native Turkana, made crayon drawings of planes and sold them to pilots.

CONTENTS

INTRODUCTION

Whenever pilots congregate the *hangar flying* begins. One pilot will mention the time the turbine wheel blew up in the engine and a piece of hot turbine blade came through the side of the cabin and embedded in his leg. The next pilot tells about the time he ran out of gas at night, over water, and ditched near a boat and was able to extricate himself from the sinking, upside down airplane and swim to the nearby boat. Two beers later another pilot tells about the time a passenger got airsick and there were no sic-sacs in the seat pocket ahead of him, so he had to use his hat. Three beers later another pilot added that he had a passenger once that didn't have a hat or sic-sac and used his shoe. Not to be outdone, another grimly remembered the time that a passenger sitting behind the copilot's seat projectile vomited across his right shoulder, the instrument panel and windshield. The sick passenger had obviously been eating something red before the flight. All this talk and beer made someone else suggest that another subject might be in order and they began talking about who had the biggest load of ice on a stormy winter night.

The stories will continue, some embellished, some true and some just plain fantasy, until the beer runs out, the wife calls and says, "get your ass home", the bar closes or the "eight hours between bottle and throttle" rule applies. One thing psychologists, sociologists or scientists have never been able to figure out is how, in a huge room full of total strangers, the pilots will soon find each other and end up in a far corner *hangar flying.* Many pilots who have their own plane will have a corner of their hangar outfitted with the aeronautical equivalent of a "man cave", consisting of an old couch and a small fridge full of beer, for use *after* flying, of course. The walls are usually decorated with pictures of P-51 fighters or antique airplanes, old *Playboy* calendars, a bent prop and have a toolbox in the corner. If the weather is too bad for flying, these hangars are the next best thing to actually getting out on the runway and trying to defy gravity. They are the ultimate location for hours of *hangar flying.*

So, being a pilot with about thirty-five years of flying, I also want to tell some stories. Why? Nobody knows for sure – that's just what pilots do! There have been hundreds, perhaps thousands of books written by pilots who want to share their love of flying but it's not about themselves, it's about **us**. It has been said that pilots are just *plane* people with a special air about them.

CHAPTER 1
IN THE BEGINNING - - -

I was born in Southern California in 1941. We were surrounded by aircraft manufacturers named Lockheed,

Friend Johnny Brookhyser watches as "Spruce Goose" is transported from Culver City to Long Beach (June 6, 1946)

North American, Douglas, Convair, Northrop, Ryan, Hughes and others. Perhaps it was this atmosphere that excited my friends and me whenever a plane flew over. Around the end of World War II we were already able to identify Mustangs (P-51) and Lightnings (P-38) and within a few years the roar of Saber jets (F-86) and Shooting Stars (P-80) stirred our juices in such a way that we all dreamed of was becoming fighter pilots when we grew up.

Lockheed F104 and North American F86D

The first step to becoming a real airplane pilot was to become a model airplane pilot. The basics of aerodynamics were all there — thrust, drag, lift and gravity. Unfortunately, gravity often won so we also became fairly good mechanics, repairing our balsa wood models after attempted loops, wing overs and inverted flight. Actually, even making a good landing was something to brag about! The model planes in those days were called U-control or control line planes and consisted of a handle about five inches long with two lines about thirty feet long that ran through the wing of the airplane to a bell crank in the fuselage and then to a rod that controlled the elevator. This made the plane go up and down. Because the pilot was holding the control handle, the plane flew around in circles, many circles, and by the time the plane ran out of gas the pilot was pretty dizzy, but anxious to refuel and do it again. We often flew on school playgrounds, taking off on smooth asphalt and doing most of the flying over grass, which was less destructive if we crashed. The sessions usually lasted about forty-five minutes, at which time a school authority would drive up and tell us to get our motor vehicles off school property. We'd then move to another school or unused baseball diamond.

The most basic entry level plane, bought for $3.95 plus tax, had a Cox .049 engine on a very rudimentary balsa wood model plane. The economic realities of airplane ownership soon became apparent after we had saved our meager income from months of mowing lawns and finally had the money needed to buy our first plane. It didn't come with gas, a battery or spare props (broken props usually resulted from even minor crashes) so this meant saving even longer before we could afford the equipment needed to finally fly our new airplanes. Control lines often came from mom's sewing cabinet and a piece of stick served as the control handle. Later in life (around 10 years of age) when we had paper routes and lots of money ($15 per month), we moved up to bigger engines and planes built up with glue and many tiny balsa sticks, covered with tissue paper and had fancy paint jobs. Because of all the work that went into these planes, crashes were quite demoralizing and led to drinking – buying Coca-Cola, rather than the free lemonade from Mom's icebox. This era was hard on Dad too because his work bench was now covered with very fragile balsa wood parts of model airplanes pinned to his work bench while the glue on the spars, ribs, longerons, stringers and formers was drying.

The *Long Beach Press Telegram* newspaper had annual subscription drives to get more readers and offered incentives to carriers to get "starts". The top reward, for seven new subscribers, was a flight on a United Airlines DC-3 from Long Beach to Catalina Island and return.

Douglas DC-3

After I rang many doorbells and gave many impassioned sales pitches, I finally had the 7 needed subscriptions. It's hard to describe the excitement in the weeks before that 15-minute flight. The last two days I couldn't sleep at all. We had a full plane load of 21 newspaper boys and took off through the overcast. Later, when I was in the Army, a popular song said *"Twenty-one miles across the sea, Santa Catalina is awaitin' for me, the island of romance, romance ----"* brought back memories. We landed at the little mountain top airport and 20 paperboys ran to the bus that was going to take us to the town of Avalon in 30 minutes. I used that 30 minutes to walk around that huge DC-3 and marveled at how this engineering marvel made all those 1000's of parts work in unison to defy gravity and transport us to this island in the Pacific Ocean in a matter of minutes. While I was standing there, mouth open and gawking, the captain came to the door and said "You wanna come up and look around, sonny?" He took me to the cockpit, sat in the copilot's seat and invited me to sit in his seat. It was, and still is, one of the most memorable moments in my life. He spent about twenty minutes showing me, and explaining the function of throttles, control yoke, altimeter, tachometers, rudder pedals, etc. To this day I wish I could have thanked him a thousand times more for that wonderful 20-minutes he gave to this 12-year-old paperboy.

On weekends we'd sometimes ride our bikes to the Long Beach Airport and wander around the ramp (no fences in those days) looking over the tied down Bellancas,

Stinsons, Luscombs, Cubs, 140's, Aeroncas and many others, and fantasize about someday being able to pilot one of those wonderful machines ourselves. We'd go into aircraft dealers and pick up brochures that we'd study to the point that we knew more about these planes than anyone on earth except the engineers who designed them. Then we'd stand around and watch with envy as fledgling pilots practiced take offs and landings in those planes.

One day as Mom and I were driving past an office complex I screamed "STOP, STOP, STOP" and nearly scared my poor Mom half to death. "What's the matter" she exclaimed as she screeched over to the side of the road. "Look Mom" I said, "there's a helicopter landing!"

I really wanted to be a fighter pilot or test pilot (how exciting), a bush pilot (exciting but in a different way) or an international airline pilot with maybe Pan Am or TWA (they go to exotic places). As I grew up, and up (to 6'5") some people warned me that to get an airline job you first had to get the aviation training and experience (known as hours) in the military but they wouldn't take guys over six-feet tall due to the cramped cockpits.
S- -t! Three days after graduating from high school I joined the Army to get my military obligation over with and spent two-and-a-half years in the Infantry in Frankfurt, Germany.

CHAPTER 2
GETTING STARTED

After getting discharged from the Army in June, 1962, the first order of business was to get a car. A 1957 Plymouth Savoy hardtop, with a 318 V-8, four-barrel carburetor, twin pipes, big fins that resembled vertical stabilizers on an airplane and three speed stick transmission, took most of my Army savings, but it was cool! It smoked a little and the transmission seemed a little sloppy, but it really looked sooooo kool. Then I got a job on the swing shift at Autonetics division of North American Aviation doing quality control work on printed circuits for ICBM's. Boring, but it paid $1.91 per hour and left the days free to attend Long Beach City College and start thinking about flying lessons.

'57 Plymouth Hardtop

FIRST LESSON: The first lesson in my logbook was on March 3, 1963 in an early model Cessna 150 without adjustable seats. The exhilaration of actually controlling a plane myself is hard to describe and the view from the cockpit was incredible. We practiced trimming the plane, climbs, glides and turns. During the excitement of that first lesson I hadn't noticed that my legs were getting numb and after the one-hour lesson, when I stepped out of that little trainer I fell to the ground. Within a few minutes feeling returned to my legs but obviously I needed to look around and find a plane whose airframe fit my frame. I went around to different flight schools in the area trying their trainers on for size and finally found one at Torrance airport. It was a somewhat weird looking fabric covered plane called an Aeronca 7FC "Tri-Champ".

Most planes of that era had the main wheels up front and a smaller third wheel in the back and were called conventional landing gear or taildraggers. About this time manufacturers finally figured out that tricycle landing gears were actually easier to land and began to switch the third wheel around to the front of the airplane, the tricycle landing gear. Many manufacturers were now starting to build new, modern designs out of aluminum whereas others just swapped the wheels around on their old, proven, fabric covered designs resulting in a strange looking plane that had no visual appeal at all but the Aeronca Tri-Champ fit my frame and flew, so I began taking lessons there. Then the transmission on my car blew resulting in a financial drain that interrupted my flying lessons for a while. This gap in lessons meant having to relearn things that I'd forgotten in the intervening time. Finally, I was back on track taking flying lessons as finances allowed when the engine on my car blew. After rebuilding the engine, I sold the kool looking Plymouth and got a mechanically sound 1956 Chevy with a six-cylinder engine and automatic transmission. Very boring but reliable. Also, about that time I met a very cute young lady and the flying lessons got put on the back burner again.

Jumping ahead to 1966, I was now married to that beautiful young lady named Rica, moved to Bellingham, Washington, was a land surveyor, and had a great little baby girl. We bought a rundown old house at Lake Samish that needed major repairs, but the dream of flying still lurked in the hidden recesses of my brain. One of Rica's brothers-in-law was an electrician in California, had a plane, about four-hundred hours of flying time and thought he'd take a shot at flying for the airlines. He already had his commercial pilots license and instrument rating, but most pilots then started out as flight engineers, so he went to a flight engineer ground school. At the end of the class an airline representative approached the class and said, "Anyone who wants to work for Alaska Airlines, follow me." He was hired and started out as a flight engineer on a Lockheed Constellation. If he could do it, without all that military training people had warned me about, why couldn't I? Actually, get paid to fly an airplane!

FIRST SOLO TO PRIVATE: In 1967 the Veterans Administration decided to allow commercial flight training as part of the G.I. veterans benefits package but what a quandary. I now had a house, a mortgage, a wife, a baby and another on the way, and steady job, and to qualify for flight training benefits you already had to first have a private pilot license. The V.A. then paid 80% of the cost towards a commercial pilot license and associated ratings.

I looked at flight schools in the area and found a small one called Floathaven at Lake Whatcom where I could get my private pilot license on wheels and floats for $500, cash. The owner/ instructor, Lane Older, took me up in a Piper Cub on floats just to make sure I fit okay. We flew around some of the most beautiful scenery in the country and then he talked me down to my first landing.

Actually, it was fairly easy to land on a thirteen-mile-long lake and I was hooked. I paid $500 cash for the private pilot training on wheels and floats so I could go flying whenever I had the time (not just the money) and it went fairly quickly.

First solo in this 85 hp Piper J-3 "Cub" on floats

Most fledgling pilots remember the anxiety and trepidation of their first solo flight. What if something went wrong? Who's going to help me get this thing (and me) back on the ground in one piece? My instructor was one of those old timers who believed that by *putting the pressure on* was how a student learned how to handle real emergency situations. He yelled and screamed and shut off the fuel and had many other uncomfortable scenarios up his sleeve, which were supposed to make us better pilots. My first solo was one of peace and elation and euphoria. No yelling or scary stuff, just me, one with that Piper Cub doing whatever I wanted. He had told me to just stay up for fifteen minutes and shoot a few touch and goes (landings and take offs) and was a little put out when I hadn't returned after thirty minutes. When I finally did taxi up to the dock he was waiting for me with a large pair of scissors. "Oh no!" I thought. He's going to cut up my student pilot license for not following orders and tell me to never come back. When I got out on the dock he told me to lift up my shirt and cut out the back of my tee shirt. Weird punishment for my transgression but I had no idea that this was an old tradition for new pilots returning from their first solo flight.

The Cub had an upgraded 85-horsepower engine but no electrical system or radios, just the raw essentials. To start the plane, you had to push off the dock and then, while standing on the right float, pull the prop through till the engine started, then as the plane taxied out into the lake, duck under the lift strut and climb into the back seat. The pilot flew a Cub from the back seat for center-of-gravity reasons. I'll throw the definition of *experience* in at this point. It's *a series of non-fatal mistakes*.

One time after starting the engine I was climbing into the plane and accidentally hit the throttle with my knee and the engine went to full power while I was hanging on and still half outside the plane. "I'll never do that again!" (*experience!*).

For practicing landing on runways, and radio and instrument work we used a new Cessna 172. We did much of that at the Bellingham airport because the strip at Floathaven was pretty rough and short. One time, after a rain, we were taxiing to the far end of the Floathaven strip to take off downhill and got stuck in the mud. I (the student) had to get out and push while Lane sat in the plane and applied full power. Naturally the prop blast covered me with mud and when I stopped at the grocery store on the way home to pick up some milk, people looked at me and said, "What on earth happened to you?" I replied "Oh, I just had a flying lesson."

Muddy runway at Floathaven

My instructor had been an enlisted pilot in the Navy during WW II and was one of the most accomplished hangar flying pilots I ever knew. One really memorable story was about the time he was flying a plane load of Aussies between islands somewhere in the South Pacific. They had taken off in a C-47 (military DC-3) and reached cruising altitude. The plane was all trimmed up and the co-pilot was already taking a nap. Suddenly the plane started into a gentle dive and Lane re-trimmed the plane and began to relax again. A couple minutes later the plane began to climb. Hmm! He looked outside to see if there was any convective activity (up and down drafts) but all was calm, but then the plane started into another dive. He woke his co-pilot up and asked him what he was doing. "Nothing, why?" After a few more up and down cycles he told the co-pilot to take over and went back into the cabin. The Aussies had set up a dart board on the forward bulkhead and they would all walk forward to tally up the score and then all walk to the back of the cabin to throw again, changing the pitch trim of the aircraft each time.

The fuel tank on a Cub is located just ahead of the windshield and the fuel gauge is a cork with a wire coming off the top which runs through a hole in the fuel cap. This system is *almost* fool proof. With a full tank the cork floats high and about 5" of wire are showing and it slowly descends as fuel is burned off. On one of the solo cross-country flights required for the private license, I was amazed at how little fuel we (the plane and I) had used until we hit a little turbulence. Suddenly the fuel indicator dropped to a very low indication. The wire was a little rusty and rough and had gotten hung up on the hole in the fuel cap till the turbulence broke it free. We made it back but there was some anxiety.

A few years after I'd moved on, I came back for a little visit and Lane told me the Cub that I'd made my first solo flight in had been wrecked. "What happened?" I exclaimed. Well, his teen aged son had been out flying it and saw a girl sunbathing in her yard and dropped down for a better look and was so distracted he didn't notice a tall cottonwood tree in front of him. He ripped off the left wing and the plane did a half roll and then hit a large fir tree inverted, head on. The plane stopped abruptly, and gravity took over (it always does) and the plane slid slowly down the trunk snapping all the branches off on the south side of the tree until he hit the ground, upside down. Fortunately, his son was unhurt but explained that he *then* lost control of the plane. They say a Cub is one of the safest planes around – it can just barely kill you.

Flying off the water is probably the next best thing to an orgasm. The door on a Cub has two halves, one folds up and the other down and in warm weather you can fly with the door open. The view is incredible and you're at one with nature, like ducks and geese, flying along wooded shorelines and beaches and able to land just about anywhere (on water, of course), but after I had my private license it was time to move on.

COMMERCIAL FLYING SCHOOL: In the mid 60's United Airlines was running ads in flying magazines looking for pilots with at least a private license and a bachelor's degree; since you started out as a flight engineer you had a year to get your commercial pilot license. I didn't have a degree but figured I could get around that somehow, after all, the plane wouldn't know the difference and my brother-in-law had done it. There were local flying schools where you could get a commercial pilots license but flying magazines were full of ads for professional schools that had structured courses that really sounded great. After talking around, I found out about Herrod Aviation, a flying school in Billings, Montana that had a good relationship with Northwest Airlines. Between 1965 and 1967 graduates from this school were going directly to work for Northwest Airlines with a fresh commercial and 250 hours of flight time. It wasn't Pan Am or TWA, but Northwest would do. We sold our house, packed our meager belongings into a trailer and moved to Billings in July, 1968.

The course lasted six months and we graduated with a commercial pilot license with instrument and multi-engine ratings, certified instrument and flight instructor ratings, advanced and instrument ground instructor ratings, and 250-hours of flight time. Classes ran from 8 AM till 8 PM and flying was any time between 6 AM and 10 PM and we had Sundays off. Basically, we lived, breathed and slept aviation, which was just fine with us. We could barely get enough of it, but it was dead serious

– not much hanger flying. All the other students in my class were *ab initio* (starting from scratch) and I remember one student coming in from his first solo flight proclaiming "Guess what? I'm now able to leap tall buildings in a single bound!" His first solo landing must have been a pretty good bounce.

BUILDING TIME: The days of getting an airline job with 250-hours were waning following the hiring binge of 1965 – 1968 so we were prepping to get jobs as flight instructors until we had the 1000-hours that most airlines now seemed to be requiring. Experience requirements for airline pilots just got down to the basics of economics – supply and demand. By the early 1970's (when demand was very low) they were requiring the eyesight of an eagle, a PhD in aeronautical engineering, 7500 hours, three moon landings and under age 24.

We finished flying school just before Christmas '68 loaded up a trailer again and headed back to Long Beach, thinking that there would be more flight instructor jobs in sunny Southern California than in Washington. Wrong, it was even slow there that winter so after a month we loaded up a trailer again and moved back to Bellingham. I needed a job and the company I'd surveyed for before hired me back, even though they realized that my heart was set on finding a flying job.

I rented planes whenever we had a little extra money and gave a little free flight instruction and diligently

19

logged those precious flight hours when a big break came along. A friend, Chuck Randall, had a son Jeff who had expressed some interest in flying and asked me if I would be interested in teaching him how to fly. I said "sure, but we need a plane". No problem, he said, "I've got a cousin in Houston, Texas who wants to sell his Cessna 171 for $4000." In May, 1971 Jeff and I took two sleeping bags and flew to Houston to pick up the plane.

The Cessna 171 was a weird duck. It was originally a 1953 Cessna 170B tail dragger that somebody had converted to a tricycle landing gear. To purists it was sacrilegious to take a beautiful plane like that and disrupt its flowing lines just to make it easier to land. When accomplished tail dragger pilots make reasonably good landings and park their planes, they don't just walk to the coffee shop – they *swagger.*

The seller of the plane worked at the NASA Space Center in Houston and gave us a personal tour of the whole facility. What a treat but the next day we took off for Bellingham.   We slept under the wings at night or in an empty nearby hangar but because of bad weather it took us over a week to get home, rather than the three days we had planned. In exchange for the instructing I got to use the plane for just the cost of the fuel. Jeff flew just fine but was not very academically inclined and when it came time for him to take his written exam, he just quit. His father figured that since he owned a plane and had an instructor at his disposal, he might as well learn to fly. It normally takes a minimum of ten hours of instruction before a student pilot is allowed to solo. Well, this particular student pilot only had about seven hours and HE decided he was ready to solo (without the required instructors okay and sign off in his logbook). The next day I was at the airport and a few people commented to me that I should have been at the airport yesterday evening. Somebody had put on quite an airshow, almost hitting a hanger, nearly going off the runway and after many attempts managed to make a multiple bounce landing back on the runway and tie the plane down. Yes, it was my fledgling student. He called that evening and confessed that he'd soloed himself. He said that's actually all he really wanted to do anyway and then quit flying. He then sold the plane to Farrokh Safavi, a professor at the local University and I taught him to fly.

During this time, we also built a small house on two acres that we had purchased at Lake Samish and I got a part time job as an instrument fight instructor at Bayview Airport, ten miles south of where we lived. It had been five-years since I had gotten my commercial pilot license and the hours were coming slowly. I was getting older, so I decided I needed to get a full-time flying job, somewhere, or be a land surveyor the rest of my life. I enjoyed surveying (except in the winter) but if I gave up my dream of flying too easily, I might have always regretted it.

Point Hope—End of the world?

CHAPTER 3
ALASKA

I came home from my surveying job one day in June 1974 and said to my wife, "Honey, take care of the house and kids, I'll be back in a year. I'm going to Alaska tomorrow to find a flying job and if I don't have enough hours to get a real flying job by then I'll settle down to surveying and quit dreaming about flying." Most less understanding wives would have probably said something such as, "Like hell you are!" but she said, with tears in her eyes "Okay, but no more than a year, and write often and let us know what you're doing."

The next day I was in Anchorage walking around Merrill Field and Lake Hood looking for a flying job, but the questions asked were not "How many hours do you have?" but "How much *Alaska time* do you have?" "Zero" was not a good answer. I became depressed at the thought of returning home empty handed. I searched newspaper ads and trade publications but to no avail except for one flight instructing job at Elmendorf Air Force Base Flying Club that didn't pay very well. This was in the middle of the Alaska Pipeline construction boom and things were outrageously expensive in Anchorage, plus I also had to send money home to pay the bills there and feed the family.

I was chatting with a pilot at a charter operation in Anchorage who felt for me and offered some friendly advice. He said to get out into the remote parts of Alaska and snoop around. Whenever those pilots get enough experience, they quit and move back to civilization, so there are more opportunities there for low time pilots. Great idea but I couldn't afford to fly all over the huge, roadless State of Alaska looking for that opening and the money I had set aside for this search was also running low. Walking down 6th Avenue looking for a cheap place to eat, I saw a Civil Engineering office. Hmmmm! I walked in and asked if they, perchance, needed a surveyor/pilot. "No, but there is another firm, over a couple blocks, that might be needing a surveyor." They needed a party chief and after a fifteen-minute interview I was hired by Bud Herschbach. The hourly pay was okay BUT they worked six days a week, twelve hours a day and paid room and board on out of town jobs. The union surveyors working on the pipe line had a higher base salary than we did, but with all the overtime and room and board I was able to send quite a bit of money home AND it gave me the opportunity to look for a flying job out where there might be more openings.

BINGO! While surveying the Native Land Claim Settlement boundary around Point Hope, on the northwest tip of Alaska, I got to know a pilot from Kotzebue who left a note that Baker Aviation in Kotzebue needed a pilot. I got word to them that I was VERY interested and would be down in two weeks. Hired

September 10, 1974! Margie Baker's husband had been killed in a bad weather accident about five years prior, but she took over running the business (though she wasn't a pilot) and raising her four kids. They had an old 6 place Cessna 206 and a new 7 place Cessna 207 and

Baker Aviation's Office in Kotzebue

three pilots, including myself. We got paid by the flying hour; in other words, no fly, no pay. No insurance, no vacation pay, no sick leave, no room and board, etc.! Therefore, we flew whenever it was possible. The flying in northwest Alaska had its good and bad days. Most of the Eskimo villages we flew to were along rivers, lakes or the coastline and easy to find in good weather but there were few navaids (navigation aids) around, so when the visibility was bad, and ceilings were low it got challenging. What we wouldn't have given for GPS, which came on-line about twenty years later and provided a 3-dimensional position right down to the ground in any weather.

My water (ice) front cabin

I rented a small one room log hut along the waterfront. It came with one light bulb on an extension cord from the neighbor's house, an oil heater, a propane stove and a five-gallon water jug which could be filled at Margie Baker's house, and that water tasted like kerosene. For showers I joined a city league basketball group and was able to shower at the school gym on Wednesday evenings after playing. The Eskimos were very quick and usually dribbled circles around me, but I was much taller than they and was occasionally able to block their shots. An Eskimo woman washed my clothes when they got too rancid, sewed traditional parkas for Rica and the girls, and made me *mukluks,* warm, knee high caribou hide footwear for the winter. As fall approached I began turning up the heat on the oil heater but when the wind blew out of the west it was still cold in the cabin due to poor chinking. One morning I woke up in my down sleeping bag with icicles in my beard and decided it was time to overhaul the carburetor on the heater. It managed to keep the cabin above freezing after that but when it got really cold outside I had to go out and shake the propane tank to stir up the molecules enough to be able to cook on my stove. *Muktuk* (whale blubber) and fish were the only locally available foods, everything else had to be flown in from Anchorage and was consequently quite expensive.

Cessna 206 on frozen river

A hunter once gave a colleague a caribou he'd shot, and he split it with me. We didn't know how to cut up meat, so we ended up with nothing resembling steaks or roasts, just gobs of meat that we froze on the porches of our huts. For cooking we carved off what we needed, chopped it up and mixed it with hamburger helper. My diet was occasionally varied by fish given to me by Eskimo passengers. One contract we had was moving a geologist camp around every few weeks. They would take water samples from rivers and creeks around their camp and then we would load up all their stuff and move them to another location. At the end of their season in the fall they gave us all their left-over food, mostly loaves and loaves of rye bread and instant pudding.

Someone's plane ran out of gas a mile from the runway. Due to fall freeze up, the plane could not be retrieved. Most of plane is submerged in a sand bar.

Ingenuity is a valuable skill in Alaska. One morning on the way to work I passed the neighbor's dog sled team staked out in the snow and noticed something out of place. It was a four-pound brick of Tillamook cheddar cheese that had been partially chewed on by the dogs. I didn't think cheese was healthy for dogs, so I took it back to my hut and cut off the chewed parts. That resulted in the invention of the now famous TUNDRA BURGER; fried, chopped up caribou on a piece of old rye bread, a slice of Tillamook cheese, sauerkraut, Dijon mustard and topped with another slice of bread. I was too intent on building up my flying hours to pursue the opportunity to make a fortune selling tundra burgers, but that possibility is still out there for someone.

Occasionally we had charters to oil drilling sites. The pilots really loved these flights because, in addition to hauling in equipment, we brought the camp their mail. This was so much appreciated that if we stopped by the mess trailer the cooks fixed us great meal with real milk, steaks, mashed potatoes, fresh salads, and desserts!

In addition to logging those valuable hours I found the flying most interesting, although the area we flew in was mostly medium mountain ranges or flat, frozen tundra. One big surprise was the Kobuk Sand Dunes which looked something like the Sahara Desert, minus the heat and camel caravans. If I was bored and had no passengers aboard I'd fly right on the deck and look at wildlife – grizzly bears, musk oxen, caribou, arctic foxes, moose, etc. Occasionally we'd call a DEW site (Distant Early Warning) on the radio and ask if they had us on radar and could give us flight following. These sites were scattered around the periphery of Alaska and were supposed to warn us of an impending nuclear attack from the Soviet Union. The one in Kotzebue must have been considered good duty since there was a village nearby but the next one north, at Cape Lisburne was at one of the most desolate places on earth; the radar guys were so eager to talk to anyone on the radio that once we called them it was hard to shake them.

In my humble opinion one of the best things about piloting an airplane is the one hundred eighty degree view out the front window. The majesty of our beautiful earth slowly passing beneath you is too profound to describe, but I'll try. A forklift was moving things around the ramp and accidentally backed into the wing of our 206. Some temporary repairs were done, and a ferry permit was issued for a flight to Anchorage for permanent repairs. The normal route was from Kotzebue to Galena, then McGrath, on through the Alaska Range and into Anchorage. It was a clear, beautiful Autumn day and fresh snow had already covered the awesome, rugged mountains of the Alaska Range as I passed through them in the late afternoon. The setting sun was casting a golden glow on the fresh snow and the more westerly peaks were casting breathtaking shadows on the more easterly mountains. I was alone but wanted to share this incredible scene with someone. My camera! Oh rats, it was in the baggage area at the rear of the cabin. I reached back as far as I could, but it was still four feet out of reach. I let go of the control wheel, took off my seat belt and leaned over the seat back as far as I could but it was still two feet out of reach and my shifting weight caused the plane to enter a climb. I pushed the control wheel forward with my foot to level the plane and sat down again. I became obsessed with capturing this once-in-a-lifetime scene and slid the co-pilot's seat forward, trimmed the nose of the plane down and wiggled to the second row of seats. The plane was climbing again and turning to the right, but I made a desperate lunge to the rear and managed to snag my camera. As I tried to climb forward the plane was in a steep right bank and had slowed considerably making me realize how stupid I had been. If the plane slowed and banked too much it would stall and enter a spin which would have pinned me to the side of the plane and given me a wild ride – downward! I managed to grab the pilot's seat and pull myself forward enough to reach the co-pilot's control wheel and level the plane. I was somewhat shaken when I got back into my seat but worse yet, when I brought the camera to my eye I realized that it would only capture a very small percentage of the whole scene that had so enthralled me. I put the camera down without taking a single picture, but I still have that memory.

Seeing the remoteness and culture of the Eskimo villages could be the basis for hours of discussion. I can understand indigenous people trying to maintain their culture, but it is not compatible with the contemporary society, technology and economics of the United States. They were traditionally subsistence hunters and had no economic base, so their lives were heavily subsidized by the BIA. The Native Land Claim settlement was supposed to help address that problem. They were given total control of lands that they could prove were historically used by them and a few billion dollars to set up enterprises to develop a local economic base. Some Native and Village Corporations have done quite well while others floundered.

Whenever we landed at an outlying village it was often difficult to get the door open because of all the people surrounding the plane to see who or what was inside. Phones were nonexistent or horribly expensive (there were shortwave radios to the hospital in Kotzebue for emergencies) so pilots were often handed notes to call into the public radio station in Kotzebue to post something on the "tundra telegraph". It was a segment broadcast several times a day with messages to everyone within a hundred miles saying that Charlie Ogert was going from Noorvik to Kiana next Thursday to see Uncle Robert, who was ailing, or some such message. No secrets up there! When I had to wait for my passengers at a village one day a bow-legged (this was often caused by rickets, due to poor diet) old Eskimo lady came up to me and started asking me where I was from and about my family. She said, "We like to get to know our pilots up here". After thinking about it, they really did rely on *their* bush pilots up there. We were their only link to the outside world unless they wanted to take a dog team or snow mobile for 300-miles to the nearest road.

Evenings were often spent at the Nu-luk-vic Inn, a hotel and restaurant about two blocks down the waterfront. There I used the restroom and then went to the bar where all the other pilots gathered at a big table in the corner for hanger talk and nursing one very expensive beer per evening. We were competitors by day but the stories and camaraderie there in the evenings was invaluable in helping new pilots survive. One night when we got together, the topic of conversation was the big white patch on the side of Gene Joiner's old green fabric covered Piper PA-12. He had a jade mine at Dahl Creek and used his plane to fly to Kotzebue for groceries. He was missing patches of hair and his fingertips from frostbite after a winter crash, was always covered with dust from his mine and couldn't take passengers with him due to a bad heart though he always brought his little black and white dog. When he arrived and was asked about the patch on his plane he slowly explained in his very dignified Georgia accent, "I've had this grizzly commin' about my mine tearin' things up so I shot him the other night but only wounded 'em. Guess he was a little pissed off at me and took it out on my plane, rippin' off some fabric on the right side so I jess soaked an ol' bed sheet in water and froze it over the hole in the plane." He said he didn't use the heater, flying to Kotzebue that day. A few weeks later the patch was larger, even covering the back window. Same bear! Same type of repair!

In looking back through logbook #2, most of the flights had no extra notations, i.e., a routine flight but some had cryptic notes like "poor Wx" (weather), "couldn't land", "white out" or "x wind". I remember that one. It was at Deering, at the south end of Kotzebue Sound. The runway was a curved patch of sand along the beach and a strong onshore wind was blowing. I touched down with full crossed controls to compensate for the cross wind when a gust hit me, and the 206 Cessna weather vanned into the wind and just hopped sideways down the runway until it stopped. Fortunately, no damage.

Another one - "2 ov 2 mi" meaning 200' ceiling with two miles visibility. Flying that low the best bet was to take a compass heading that would intersect a river somewhere downstream from the village you were going to and then follow the river upstream till you found the village. Some of the rivers, especially the upper Kobuk, were crooked as a dog's hind leg, which made following them at low altitude extremely challenging. The river valley was surrounded by 6000' mountains, so you absolutely couldn't lose sight of the river and you were flying so low you feared for dipping a wingtip into the water at a sharp curve.

Another one, "8 inches snow at Kobuk". Had to pick up four passengers. Tracks were visible in the snow so apparently the runway was in use. Just before touchdown it was clear that the snow was pretty deep for a wheeled plane, but it was too late. We stopped in about 300-feet; had we been in a taildragger we surely would have flipped over on our back. The passengers were waiting at the other end of the runway, but it took almost full power just to taxi there. How would we take off? I told them that I doubted we'd be able to take off, but we'd try. No luck, there was just too much drag to get flying speed. The other tracks were from a Twin Otter turboprop with huge tires and a ski plane. If we couldn't get the runway plowed or packed down, we'd be there for a long time, but I had one last ditch idea. If we could lighten our load, maybe, just maybe, we could get out of there. I put one passenger in the back seat to help get the nose wheel out of the snow and tried another take off with full flaps. At low altitude and -35 degrees temp, the engine was putting out more than normal rated power and we managed to plow out of there and fly to Dahl Creek, a plowed strip about 20 minutes away. I dropped the passenger off and flew back to Kobuk for another extremely short field landing. After 4 round trips we had them all together at Dahl Creek for the trip back to Kotzebue. The first passenger was quite cold from waiting and asked for full heat!

At that time some of the Eskimos in the area had picked up good paying jobs on the Alaska pipeline – home a month and gone a month. About 60% of our business was flying these Eskimos back and forth to their villages from Kotzebue and the rest was hauling anything that would fit in the plane – barrels of gasoline, dead seals, dog teams, government workers, propane tanks, troopers with their prisoners, oil drilling bits, etc.

The days around the autumnal equinox in the Arctic get shorter by over half an hour each day and this caught me by off guard when Margie asked if I had enough time to get to Shungnak and I said, "sure". Well, it was dark by the time I got there and there were no runway lights. I knew approximately where the runway was in relation to the lights in the village but after multiple low passes with

35

my landing lights on, could never get lined up enough to land. Finally, a guy in the village heard the racket and came out with his snow mobile and parked it at one end of the runway with the light on and walked to the other end with a flashlight to guide me in.

Business was slowing down with the approaching winter and Leon Shellabarger, an old-time polar bear guide turned charter pilot, offered me a job in February, when he got back from Hawaii. What a deal, I could quit Baker and be home with the family for the holidays. Shellabarger provided housing in his former lodge for

the pilots - with well heated rooms, a shower and a place for me to set up a basic kitchen made from *Blazo boxes*. These were highly sought-after wooden boxes, about 10"X20" and 14"high that held two 5-gallon cans of Blazo, white gasoline that was used in Coleman stoves and lanterns. They could be stacked up in various configurations to make quite practical cabinets. A single burner electric hotplate was perfect for fixing my simple meals.

Leon had a Cessna 180 & 206 and a Piper Navajo twin. I was really looking forward to flying the Navajo and logging that multi-engine time but the insurance required more than my paltry 6.8 hours so I had to fly with his part time multi-engine pilot for free, whenever it could be fit in. That didn't work out as well as I'd hoped, only picking up a few twin-engine flights but did get quite a bit of time in the Cessna 180 taildragger mounted on wheel-skis. If landing on softer snow the skis could be lowered.

Cessna 180 on wheel-skis

Piper Navajo

By this time everything was white – the rivers and lakes were frozen over and the villages were covered with snow. More than once I flew right by a village without seeing it and when it was obvious that we should have been there, had to turn around and make another pass.

Shellabarger's airport office

Kotzebue hosted a northwest Alaska high school basketball tournament that winter and afterward I had a charter to fly five of the cheer leaders back to Bethel, about two hours south. Fortunately, all travelers in Alaska dress warm in the winter because about ten minutes after takeoff it was still rather cold in the airplane. After messing with the heater control it became apparent that it was either frozen shut or something was broken but we continued on to Bethel anyway. It was cold but tolerable, but there was another problem. With six people breathing in such a confined space, everyone's breath was freezing to the windows making visibility very difficult. I couldn't tell my passengers to stop breathing so the only other solution I could think of at the moment was to scrape the ice off the inside of the windows every five minutes with my Chevron credit card. It worked!

Eskimo spring baseball

Unfortunately, many Alaska natives drank excessively. This caused many problems and some Boroughs (Counties) had made themselves "dry", not allowing alcohol. We were occasionally approached by natives to bring them a couple cases of *hooch* at a pretty good profit. I'm no saint but after seeing the social and health problems it caused, I couldn't do it.

One evening, just as I was tying the plane down, Leon came out and asked if I wanted to make one more flight. "Sure". Three very drunk passengers staggered out to the plane and we buckled the two worst ones into the middle seats of the 206. Leon asked the third one for the fare, but he said the one already buckled in had all their money. Leon asked him repeatedly for the fare, but he just mumbled he wanted to go home and some obscenities. Leon finally grabbed the would-be passenger under the armpits and yanked him out of the seat back, over his shoulder, out the back door of the plane and headfirst into the snow. Never underestimate the strength of an angry man. Unfortunately, as he came flying out of the seat, the seat belt stripped his pants down to his ankles and his hand, clutching all the money, released it when he hit the ground and the cash went flying all over the ramp. We gathered up several hundred dollars for them and Leon said, "Put the plane away Rich and you guys come back tomorrow when you've sobered up a little". Leon helped me plug the plane heaters in, tie it down and as we were driving home saw the two guys dragging the third, face down, through the snow. He stopped and asked them where they were going. He picked up the drunkest one and threw him into the back of the snow-filled pickup truck and told the other two to climb up. As we headed to where they were staying in town Leon explained his humanitarian gesture. "If you leave 'em out here they freeze to death, then you've got no more customers". A few days later I was talking to a guy who kept his Super Cub tied down on the ice off the end of the runway and he told me that as he was untying his plane that morning there was a $20-dollar bill wrapped around the tie down rope.

Another memorable night, Leon asked if I wanted to take a couple guys to Selawik, which had a beacon and runway lights but was fairly short with a river at one end but no other obstructions. "Sure". We buckled them into the center row of seats, and I took up a compass heading, expecting to pick up the rotating beacon in about 40 minutes. About halfway to Selawik I felt some movement behind me and suddenly one of the passengers flopped over the copilot's seat back and into the control wheel, sending the plane into a momentary dive. After straightening things out I exclaimed, "What the hell are you doing?" "Me help you fly". I told him that I didn't need any help, but he insisted, saying that all other pilots let him fly. Rather than risking a confrontation I said okay but maintain 2000-feet and heading 160 degrees. It was a black night, snowing lightly and without a visible horizon or lights on the ground, it is physically impossible to keep the plane level without knowing how to read the instruments, so shortly we were in a spiral decent. I recovered to straight and level and severely chastised my "helper", but he wanted to try again. After the third try he grunted "You fly". At this point we should have been able to see the beacon or other lights at Selawik when he mumbled something about the generator at the village being out. "Crap' I said, 'If you knew this, why did you want to fly out here tonight?" He said, "Maybe they put lanterns on runway for me". Sure enough, as we got closer I could make out some dim lights in the village and four kerosene lanterns about where the runway should have been, presumably at each end of the runway. Using the plane's landing lights in snow just causes a blinding glare so I waited till just before touchdown at the first two lanterns before turning them on. We were already over the runway, so I pulled the power off and landed, but the other end of the runway was coming up real fast and the brakes weren't doing too well on the packed snow. All I could do at this point was hit full left rudder and skid the plane sideways. We stopped about 30 feet from the end of the runway and the river. My legs were a little wobbly when I got out of the plane but when a local guy came up I asked him if those two lanterns were at the other end of the runway. He said, "Oh no, they blow out, those are in the middle" (of an already short runway).

Expect the unexpected! One evening I had to fly to Noorvik and pick up a whole planeload of large propane cylinders and take them to Kiana, which had runway lights. It was a cold, clear night, about 30 below and the *aurora borealis* were out bright. Downright enchanting, but shortly after takeoff I noticed a smell. One of the propane tanks was leaking! The thought of the gas exploding if I flipped a switch or keyed the mike crossed my mind, so I opened the window and let that clear, **cold** air in. Fortunately, I could zip up my parka and put on my big mittens but by the time I landed at Kiana I had icicles in my whiskers again.

The next morning, as I was fixing my breakfast Leon came to my room and said I had a call from some guy named Bud from Anchorage. It was my surveying boss, wondering if I'd like to go back to work for him as a corporate pilot flying a Piper Aztec twin and surveying when I wasn't flying.

Piper Aztec

I had just gotten comfortable flying for Leon and was planning to have the family come up for the summer to see *real* Alaska and then head home the following winter, so I turned the new job offer down. Then he said the salary would be $60,000 a year (probably $250,000 in today's money). WOW, but I said no again. He said, "Think about it and call me back in a few days." When I told Leon, he said "You're crazy. I can't pay you nearly that much and you'll be logging all that multi-engine time and living in civilization. Somewhat reluctantly I called Bud back and accepted.

I packed up my stuff and flew to San Diego where I met Bud and we picked up our plane. After a checkout we flew up to Bellingham and spent the night with my family. All the plans I had for the year were now disrupted, so all I could tell Rica before we left was that I'd let her know when things settled down and I had a new plan. We flew to Anchorage the next day and I began looking for a place to live. HA! There were no apartments or rooms available in all of Anchorage due to the pipeline boom. People were even renting space to roll out a sleeping bag in the basement of the Baptist Church. After being home with the family that one night and then facing this, I apologized to Bud and said "Sorry, but I'm going home."

CHAPTER 4
ISLAND AIR

It's said that one man's misfortune is another's fortune. I was now home with the family but unemployed, still not enough hours to get a good job and in an area where flying jobs were scarce as hen's teeth. Someone told me to check out the charter service at Anacortes because he'd heard that someone down there had gotten hurt and they might need some temporary help. Sure enough, Bob Crawford, a retired Navy pilot who had bought *Island Air* and was a one plane, one man flying service, had gotten his hand pretty mangled by an airplane propeller and needed help. He had a Cessna 207 like I had flown in Alaska and did charters, primarily

to the San Juan Islands and had part of a US Postal Service contract to haul the mail to the Islands. He was just getting ready to go on the evening mail run and asked me if I wanted to go along. I said, "Sure" and then he asked if I wanted to fly. This sounded like a good opportunity strut my stuff, so off we went. He was a little nervous about riding into Shaw Island with someone who had never landed there before, since you come down between the trees, under power lines and then land up a steep hill. I didn't crash so when we got back to Anacortes he called his insurance agent and told him that he had just hired a pilot. The pay wasn't great, but I was home with the family, having a lot of fun and adding hours to my logbook.

The daily routine was fairly similar – mail run in the morning and late afternoon and charters, mainly to the San Juan Islands during the day. Four of the islands had paved runways and the rest were gravel. Some had lights and some usually had crosswinds; in the winter the fog, turbulence and low ceilings and visibility kept things interesting. Occasionally the funeral director in Anacortes would charter us to pick up a body and once we had to fly out over the Pacific Ocean to dump ashes. He was a bit of a strange duck and when I asked if we should take along a tube to stick out the back door to dump the ashes into he just told me to fly the plane – he knew how to dump ashes. You would also think a funeral director would have a fairly strong stomach but the first thing he did was get out a sic-sac and right after takeoff began filling it, and not with old Charlie's ashes. I signaled him when we got three miles out over the Pacific and as he propped open the back door I could feel quite a swirl of wind coming into to the plane. Suddenly it was like a dust storm. Old Charlie was in my hair (which I had in those days), down my shirt and on the instrument panel and seats. When we got back to Anacortes I swept about half of old Charlie out onto the ramp, but I doubt that his relatives got a refund.

Occasionally I would take our kids to work with me and if there were empty seats, they could ride along. They really liked the mail run though. The Cessna 207 had a fairly long fuselage and when the plane was empty they'd say, "Make me float, Daddy". If you pull the nose up fairly steeply and then push it over into a parabolic arc, everything not tied down becomes weightless. They'd take their seat belt off and as the plane accelerated under them they would float to the back of the plane. Thunk! When they hit the back bulkhead, I'd level off and they would run to the front and say, "Do it again, Daddy".

The islands without ferry service have a *school boat* that took the few kids that lived on them to a bigger island that had schools. One winter a high school girl on Blakely Island needed to get to school before the school boat came for an extracurricular activity and the boss arranged for me to pick her up on the morning mail run to Eastsound on Orcas Island. Blakely had a paved strip and lights but was oriented in such a way that during a northeast wind you had a tailwind whichever way you landed. I remember landing in the dark during a northeaster with a heavy load of mail to pick her up and braking so hard the brake disks were glowing red.

Weekends in the summer really got busy hauling people back and forth, mainly to the islands that weren't served by the ferries. They were just short hops from Anacortes and one Sunday I made 36 landings in 4.6 hours of flying time. The boss recognized the inefficiency of using the big 207 if there were only two passengers and leased a 4 place Cessna 172 for light loads. The word also spread that there was a flight instructor (me) on the field and I began picking up flight students too. Before long I had 1000 hours and then 1200 hours. I had also gotten to know the San Juan Airlines pilots with whom we shared the mail contract. About the time Bob Crawford decided to sell Island Air the chief pilot at San Juan Airlines offered me a job.

CHAPTER 5
SAN JUAN AIRLINES

Passengers who flew into Sea-Tac Airport on a regular airline were often quite surprised by what they were getting onto next. San Juan Airlines had a hodgepodge of small piston-engine aircraft ranging from 4 place Cessna 172's to 7 place 207's and the queen of our fleet, a 10 place, twin engine Britten-Norman Islander. Oh, we even had a 1938 Stinson SR-10E which was used for hauling the mail. The pilots had no uniforms and often wrote out the tickets and collected the money themselves at the outlying stops but, we were listed in the Official Airline Guide and got pass benefits with many of the large airlines. It had grown in fits and starts to fulfill the need for air service to the Islands after WW II as Orcas Island Air Service.

Roy Franklin, a former Navy pilot, acquired it in the late 1940's and it became Island Sky Ferries and later San Juan Airlines. Roy ran a tight ship – he had to. When I went to work for him in 1976, the fare from the Islands to Bellingham or inter-island flights was $10 and to Sea-Tac, $25. Roy was more committed to serving the residents of the Islands than he was to making money; his book, *Island Bush Pilot,* makes this pretty obvious. A raise in fuel prices, a few days of bad weather or a major repair would have caused most people many sleepless nights or serious ulcers, but he was there every day micro-managing things and making them run as efficiently as possible. I understood this and in spite of getting chewed out regularly when he was in a bad mood, we became good friends.

For some reason Roy began letting me fly the old Stinson on the mail run, which was quite an honor since the old bird was his personal pet. She was a big taildragger and had a "Bushman" conversion with a smokin', snarlin' 450 horsepower Pratt & Whitney radial engine on the front and a stretched fuselage.

Stinson SR-10E, "Bushman" conversion

She did nice barrel rolls but every once in a while she'd do something to scare you and show you who's boss. Roy used to chastise us if he suspected we were doing aerobatics with the planes because "it was hard on the gyros". One summer evening I was flying a 207 back from an ambulance run to Bellingham and had to stop at Orcas Island to drop off the stretcher. Roy was at the other end of the field chatting with a bunch of friends and hadn't noticed me land. When he got ready to leave I taxied up behind him planning to fly formation with him back to Friday Harbor, but he headed north in a steep climb, so I just followed at a safe distance. Then he turned south and flew over his buddies and did three loops in a row. When he finally headed towards Friday Harbor I pulled up next to him and waved. After we put the planes away he came over and asked how long I'd been following him. I said," I saw the whole show, Roy." He just grinned and walked away

Roy's wife, Margret Ann and his brother Dale were dispatchers and their sons, Steve and Kenny, were pilots when they weren't away in the Army or college. Most of the other pilots were retired and flew just for the joy of it or building time, hoping to get a big airline job.

As there were no jails or hospitals in the Islands, a dispatcher and pilot were on duty 24/7 for emergency flights to a mainland ambulance or county jail. We eventually got used to the phone ringing at 3 AM but at first it was rather unnerving to be woken up at all hours and told to hurry to the airport and get a 172 or 207 ready for an emergency or sheriff's flight to Bellingham, Oak Harbor or Seattle. Many times, around town, we'd be approached by a woman who would introduce us to their small baby saying that, "You were the pilot who flew me to Bellingham that stormy night last week to have our new baby". Made one feel kind of special although I've often wondered why women waited till midnight to have their babies. Another time it was for a commercial diver who had the bends and had to be flown to Seattle for decompression. Because altitude would have exasperated the problem we had to fly low and it was a surprised air traffic controller when I reported in at 500' over Puget Sound in the middle of the night. We put a lot of faith in Lycoming and Continental engines and the mechanics who kept them running, although it's often said that engines go into "automatic rough" over mountains or water, especially at night.

One rainy winter afternoon I got a call from dispatch to go to Crane Island and pick up an injured pilot. No other details. The airstrip at Crane was flat with no obstructions at either end but was only 1300' long, grass and had sharp drop-offs at both ends. As I was on short final I saw a Piper Cherokee on the rocks just above the waterline off the west end of the runway. A guy with a somewhat bloodied face met me on the runway and on the way to the Bellingham hospital told me what happened. He kept his plane at Paine Field, where the Boeing 747's were made and they had a 9000' runway. He wanted to "practice" short field landings, so he found the shortest runway on the chart to practice, Crane Island. In aviation you normally practice someplace that allows you an out if you make mistakes, until you can do it right every time because mistakes in tight situations are usually unforgiving. The first two times he tried to land, he overshot the runway completely but on his third try he touched down midfield and when he hit the brakes he just skidded on the wet grass. By the time he recognized he wouldn't get stopped before the drop-off at the end he was going too slow to takeoff and go around and plunged to the rocks below. He was lucky he only wrecked his plane.

Sheriff flights were sometimes quite interesting. We wouldn't talk to the deputy with a shackled prisoner on board on the way to jail but on the way back we'd get all the juicy details. Late one summer evening I had to pick up a deputy and prisoner on Lopez Island who really smelled of alcohol. On the way back the deputy said that he was at home sitting in his recliner, watching TV when he heard a crash in his front yard, so he walked outside and arrested the drunk driver who had hit his oak tree. San Juan Island finally built a jail and it was quite a relief not to have to make those flights, until one night the dispatcher called and said, "Sheriff's flight from Friday Harbor to Oak Harbor". I tried to argue that we weren't making those flights anymore, but he said the sheriff was quite adamant. The prisoner was quite a big guy and was ONLY wearing a strait jacket and chains around his ankles. He was also quite drunk and on the flight back the disgruntled deputy explained what had happened. He had arrested the guy for drunk driving and hauled him in to spend the night in their brand-new jail. They had him disrobe completely and gave him some orange jail cloths to wear but he refused to put them on, so they threw him and the orange cloths in the cell and locked it. Apparently the prisoner didn't like being in there either and backed up to the far wall. He then ran full speed and hit the door, ripping it completely out of the wall of their new jail. It took two deputies to get him into the straight jacket and that's the way they brought him to the airport. Thank god it was 2 AM and dark.

Britten-Noman BN-2A "Islander"

Being surrounded by water, as islands usually are, opened the door for many charter flights to places not served by the ferries or scheduled flights. These flights were sometimes very interesting but the best were giving scenic flights. Being in one of the most beautiful parts of the country with many tourists coming through, it was natural that some wanted to see it from the air, and I remember one in particular. They were a very beautiful, classy looking woman, about 30, and her daughter, about 6. They wanted a half-hour scenic flight. I asked if they wanted to see anything in particular and the mother just said no. It was a beautiful late Spring day with clear blue skies, scattered, puffy clouds and the snowcapped mountains in the distance. First we flew low up the west side of San Juan Island looking at the rugged shoreline and I pointed out some bald eagle nests and we circled a pod of Orcas headed south through Haro Straights. Then we climbed and flew past the lookout tower on top of Mt. Constitution, waving at the tourists as we flew by and then began our descent back towards Friday Harbor. The woman said nothing throughout the flight, as if enraptured by the beauty of the scene around us, but then she spoke. "Could we stay up another half hour?" I called the office and they said no problem. The little girl had taken off her seat belt and was excitedly scooting from one side window on the back seat to the other, so as not to miss a thing and then she tapped her mother on the shoulder and whispered something in her ear. The mother said to me, "My daughter was wondering if we could fly through a cloud?" I said, "Sure, which one." She pointed, "That one." After we exited out the other side, she squealed with excitement, "Mommy, mommy! It was just like the inside of a glass of milk." What greater joy could a pilot have than that?

After flying around the Islands for a while, some characteristics of the residents of the various islands became apparent - Blakely was affluent, Lopez was agricultural, Waldron was hippy-ish, San Juan was artsy, etc. When a new gravel runway was built on Waldron, some residents there planted trees in the middle of the runway to keep planes from landing. It's suspected that a lot of pot was being grown there.

Stuart Island had an old Chippewa Indian who kept everybody laughing. His name was Little Wolf, who claimed his parents died when he was a baby and he was raised by wolves. He also claimed that Al Capone had taught him how to drive and during prohibition he came west and used to run booze from Victoria to Anacortes in a high-speed boat. Once a month, when he got his Social Security check, he'd take the mail plane back to Friday Harbor to do his monthly shopping. That evening, the pilot on the last Bellingham run had to hit all the bars in town to find Little Wolf, load up his big pile of groceries, help him into the plane and take him back to Stuart Island. On the way he'd try to give the pilot his remaining money claiming he had no place to spend it on Stuart anyway.

Little Wolf was famous for his copper bracelets. John Wayne wore one and when Betty Ford was on the cover of *Newsweek* magazine she had one on. I took my family and an exchange student from Thailand to the cabin he shared with two dogs, a goose and some chickens once and had them fitted. He claimed they protected you from gout, shingles, rheumatism, cancer, etc. and even made the battery in his watch last twice as long. I don't know if the power company ever figured out where that missing roll of copper wire went. Little Wolf loved the adventure of flying but one morning on the way from Stuart to Friday Harbor he seemed a little glum, so I did a loop to cheer him up. He let out a yell that would have made any Chippewa proud. He said that someone had brought some cheap, rot gut whiskey to the island yesterday and he didn't feel so good.

In some ways living in the Islands was lots of fun and we had made many good friends there; but, living on an island was also rather confining and San Juan Airlines was not exactly a career position for a young family man. Ernest Gann, a friend who was a former American Airlines pilot wrote a letter for me but the chief pilot at American replied that to be competitive I should have my Airline Transport Pilot license. I rented the Britten-Norman twin and had a friend give me intense instruction on regulations and emergencies and called the FAA to set up an appointment for the check ride. The inspector was a former Tuskegee Airman named Chuck Copper and when we sat down for the oral he looked at me with a chilling gaze and said, "ATP huh? Well you better be gooood." I almost gave up right then but after the oral we took off into a snowstorm and did all the required maneuvers, emergencies and approaches and after we landed he said, "Congratulations."

I, and many of my young colleagues, had been sending out resumes and applications but hiring was still slow. A friend, Kent Jacobson, did get a job with a commuter airline called Cascade Airways in Walla Walla and said that they were hiring. They just flew 15 passenger turboprops around the Northwest, but I wanted to fly jets internationally and hesitated. He said they're growing, and I'd be getting turbine time. Hmmm.

Embraer EMB-110 Bandeirante

CHAPTER 6
CASCADE AIRWAYS

Federal Aviation Regulations require that commercial planes carrying ten passengers, or more must have two pilots and carrying twenty passengers, or more must have flight attendants. When the need for commuter airlines, to serve short runs and outlying areas, became apparent in the 1960's, there weren't many economically viable planes available to fit these requirements. Cascade Airways started out flying 15 passenger, unpressurized Beechcraft 99 turboprops between Spokane and Seattle in the early 1970's. They weren't ideal but it was a start. When I was hired in October 1978, they had just bought another small commuter airline that was using Swearingen Metro pressurized 19 passenger turboprops. It was basically a stretched corporate plane that was so under powered that it had a rocket in its tail that could be fired if they lost an engine after takeoff to help keep it in the air until the landing gear and flaps could be cleaned up. I avoided it and flew co-pilot on the Beechcraft.

Everything in the airlines is based on seniority and experience so being a new, lowly copilot was a real learning experience. Working as a crew was new to me and it took a while to figure out how to exactly share the flight responsibilities. The flights were alternated, with one pilot flying the plane and the other handling the radio and navigation work and vice versa on the next leg. Standardization is stressed because every month you might be flying with a different pilot and everything had to mesh. Naturally, people are different and sometimes you flew with someone you worked with better than others and that was a real pleasure. A crew that meshed and worked together as a team made flying, even in the worst situations as satisfying as a sports team making a triple play in baseball or a double reverse to a touchdown in football. While flying captain on the Beech 1900 I had a new copilot and before flying we always discussed responsibilities, etc. On the last leg back into Walla Walla it was the copilot's leg, and everything had gone fine the whole day, but the weather had deteriorated to a 200' ceiling, visibility ½ mile in blowing snow – minimums! We discussed the approach and missed approach and my call outs during the ILS (Instrument Landing System). He was doing a good job of keeping the needles centered and I called out, "final approach fix, good altitude, needles centered". The ILS will take you down to 200' above the runway at which point you have to have either the runway or runway environment (runway lights) in sight. The non-flying pilot calls out the elevations and what he sees every 100' to the decision height, at which point the landing is assured or a missed approach is initiated. "400', nothing in sight, needles and gauges lookin' good – 300', slight glow (from the approach lights), 200' got the rabbit (a lead in strobe light), stay on the gauges" "You wanna land?" "100' lookin' good, stay on the gauges." Anxious tone in his voice - **"You wanna' land?"** "Minimums, I got it." After I landed and all the passengers got off the plane I asked, "What was that all about?" He confessed that he was from Arizona and had never done an actual instrument landing before, only simulated with a vision restricting hood on and when you reached the decision height you took it off and it was bright and sunny. I was a little upset but calmly tried to explain that 200' above the runway at 110 mph was not the proper time to have that discussion. "Communicate!"

Shortly after moving to Walla Walla our neighbor and former colleague from San Juan came over and excitedly told me that he had gotten a letter for an interview with Alaska Airlines and was hired two weeks later. About a week later I got a similar letter and when I called they said, "Where have you been? All the interview slots have been filled". I hadn't updated my resume and their letter was sent to Friday Harbor and took over a week to get forwarded to our new address in Walla Walla. I could have cried. Living in Walla Walla was okay. We bought a large, classic two-story house built in 1906 and began a seven-year remodel project, trying our best to preserve the old charm of the house. It was a block from Whitman College and the oldest symphony orchestra west of the Mississippi River. We made many friends there and got involved in foreign student exchange programs. At that time commercial flights were usually about two-thirds full which made traveling on space-available passes quite doable. More than once the kids would say, "Hey, spring break is coming up. Where are we going? Mexico, Europe, Hawaii?" Talk about spoiled!

Cascade was in dire need of a better commuter airliner and when Embraer of Brazil came out with a new 18 seat model, the EMB-110, we immediately bought two and I was able to bid copilot on one. It had leather seats, was roomy and quiet but was unpressurized and had a rather poor heating and air conditioning system. The pilots were allowed to wear snow boots in the winter because cold air coming in around the rudder pedals would surely have resulted in frostbite. On hot summer days we couldn't use the air conditioning on the ground or climb out because it used bleed air off the engines, which wasn't available on those two phases of flight. We also didn't have toilets. We were at 10,000' over the Eagle Cap Wilderness area in central Idaho when a young woman came to the cockpit and asked where the bathroom was. "Sorry ma'am, but we don't have one". Five minutes later she came up again and asked, "What's in the back?" "Baggage". "Can I get in there?" "No." "I gotta go". At that point the captain did all he could. He handed her a sic-sac, which she carried off the plane in Lewiston with some yellow liquid in it.

We often had "overnights" where the company wanted to have a plane situated for early morning departures. One such was in Olympia, the State capital. When we arrived there, late at night, one of our agents greeted us and said that they had good and bad news for us (the crew). "We know where your night bags are". It didn't take a rocket scientist to figure out that our overnight bags with a fresh shirt, toothbrush and razor weren't in Olympia. At our previous stop we had a plane change and we immediately put our bags in the new plane but while we were in the terminal doing paperwork a helpful baggage handler, knowing that the crew had a plane change there, put our bags back in the plane we had flown in and they ended up in Boise, Idaho. When we got to the hotel the guys at the counter thought that was the funniest thing they had ever heard. One said, "I've heard of passenger's bags being lost, but never the flight crew's. Ha-ha!" and they gave us some supplies they kept for such situations for airline passengers.

One regular overnight was in Moses Lake, a dry, rather desolate town in central Washington where Japan Airlines had a training base. Often, as we flew in we would hear a JAL DC-10 or 747 pilot in the traffic pattern talking to the tower on the radio but they were very hard to understand, although my Japanese would certainly been worse. One afternoon, as I was checking the weather, my captain was on the observation deck watching the big planes practicing landings and struck up a conversation with another guy watching. Turns out that he was an American flight instructor working for JAL and my boss asked where he learned Japanese. He remarked that he didn't speak any Japanese and my boss commented that we heard those guys on the radio.

"How can you teach someone to fly a 747 with such a language disparity". He said, "Before we get in the plane I make sure they understand two phrases - first 'I've got it' (meaning I'm taking control) and then 'Don't **EVER** do that again!'".

Hawker-Siddeley 748

By 1982 the leaders at Cascade decided they had to get bigger or drop out and bought a whole new fleet — five reconditioned BAC 111 jets, two new 50 seat and nine new 19 seat turboprops. I was copilot on the fifty seat Hawker-Siddeley 748.

Ah, pressurized and capable of flying over most of the weather, flight attendants, toilets, drinks, peanuts and a transport category aircraft. It was a new airplane with old technology. The Rolls-Royce Dart engines were horribly noisy, making an extremely loud screeching noise that nearly deafened everyone on the ramp. I asked a Rolls-Royce tech rep once why they didn't do something to quiet that engines down. He said, "Well, old John at Rolls had designed air raid sirens during the war and some of that must have carried over when he designed the compressor section of that engine. The engine was designed in 1948 and shortly thereafter jets came out and no further development was done on turboprops but now, with fuel prices going up, the efficiency of them has suddenly become important".

I was taxiing out in our little Pacer (see Chapter 16) in Walla Walla once when one of our 748's passed me going the other way. I said, "Hi guys" on the radio. A few days later I was flying with that same captain and he mentioned that the copilot he was with remarked, as we passed on the taxiway, "Look at that idiot, flying on his day off". After a little thought I realized that there were three kinds of airline pilots. (1) There were the *ego pilots*. They had shined shoes, pressed, tailored shirts and uniform, a cool haircut and usually walked through the terminal on his way to the plane rather than through the ops room and the ramp. He also had a bladder problem, necessitating him to put his hat on, walk through the cabin on each leg of a flight, smile at all the passengers and ask how the flight is going. Flight attendants didn't like them because they were always in the way during in-flight service. If they had their own plane, it was something hot and showy like a P-51 or Pitts Special.

(2) There were the *professional pilots* who had heard that flying for a big airline paid well, had a lot of time off and was highly respected. After college they joined the Air Force to fly transports and then went right to work for an airline. They had never flown small planes, didn't like them and didn't think they belonged in his airspace. And (3), there were the *enthusiast pilots* who loved flying and anything to do with aviation and were either constructing a home-built or restoring an antique airplane or flew gliders in their time off. As the monthly crew schedules changed, it didn't take long to put a new captain into one of those three categories. People are different and they could all be friendly and were competent, but it was just an interesting observation. An old lady was once talking to a pilot and remarked, "My, an airline pilot. That must be so exciting"? He replied, "No ma'am, if it's exciting we're doing something wrong".

Commercial pilots take many check rides. There is one for each license they hold, a type rating for each airplane (over 12,500 lbs.) they fly and 6-month check rides for captains and annual check rides for copilots. These are pretty intense. A group of pilots were standing around talking when one mentioned that he had a check ride coming up and was a bundle of nerves. Another said he couldn't sleep for the week before his check rides. Another said he couldn't keep food down the day before. The fourth one said that he sleeps like a baby the night before his check ride. The others looked at him in amazement until he said, "I wake up every two hours, crying". They consist of an oral and written exam where you must quickly recite memorized emergency checklists, calculate weight and balance problems and review regulations and the flight manual. Then comes the actual ride itself. They used to be done in the airplane itself which usually involved doing instrument landings with one engine shut down and weren't too bad. Now most are done in simulators where all manner of emergencies can be thrown at the sweating pilot without fear of killing anybody. If a check ride is failed, the pilot is given more training and another ride with the FAA and a union observer present; if that one is failed, you're looking for a job.

Cessna Caravan instrument simulator

Beechcraft 1900 20-passenger turboprop

I felt, at this point of my career, that I should have some captain time and bid down to our new Beechcraft 1900's. It was a 19 seat, pressurized turboprop that was one of the best flying planes that I'd ever flown, had 1200 horsepower engines and could climb right up to 25,000 feet, but not all was well. A new commuter airline, Horizon Air, had started up in our area of operations and we had taken on a tremendous debt load with all the new equipment. In the beginning Horizon had done some very unscrupulous and unethical things such as using the same flight number as Cascade's but leaving five minutes earlier. The FAA finally stepped in. Then a month of extremely bad weather around Christmas 1985 made things worse. The company began paying all employees $100 a week trying to keep things going. This went on till March 5, 1986, when all the airplanes were repossessed, and the CEO scrounged up all the liquid assets he could find and sent us all a note saying thanks for sticking with him and check for about $300.

CHAPTER 7
SAN JUAN AIRLINES, AGAIN

I got an interview with New York Air, which was owned by Frank Lorenzo, who also owned Continental Airlines, which was in the middle of a vicious labor dispute. At the interview the Director of Flight Ops told us that they expected us to commute to work since they didn't pay us enough to live in New York City. In about a week I got a DC-9 class date. Since I loved the Northwest I had planned to commute from Bellingham, but Rica insisted that we would live wherever I was domiciled. I balked and then declined the job. Those friends that did go there ended up with Continental Airlines, domiciled in Houston, Texas. Ugh! Also, had an interview with Evergreen International, a non-scheduled freight and passenger airline. They had their ups and downs (no pun intended) and at this point in my life I was looking for some stability and turned them down.

Since I had left San Juan Airlines, Roy had sold the company to Jim Sherill, a businessman from Portland who also loved airplanes. They now flew mostly nine passenger Cessna 402 twins but were looking at larger aircraft and had expanded their scheduled routes to include Portland, Port Angeles, Vancouver and Victoria.

This certainly wasn't Pan Am, but we could be living in Bellingham and flying around some of the most beautiful parts of the world. As is typical in the airline industry, I started at the bottom of the seniority and pay scale, again.

Jim was a promoter – the airplanes were all refurbished and painted alike, the pilots now wore uniforms, there were in flight magazines and we were encouraged to do whatever we could to make flying on San Juan Airlines a pleasant experience. If we saw a pod of whales, take the extra minutes to circle them, or fly down the scenic Frazer River into Vancouver. The passenger comment cards in the seat pockets were flooding in with kudos. One winter day after a storm had passed through, I asked the passengers if anyone had any tight connections in Seattle or could we take a few minutes longer and do the scenic route. It was a perfect day and they all agreed to do a scenic route. We took off from Port Angeles and flew back over Ediz Hook and then up the Elwha River valley through the Olympic Mountains. The previous day's storm had left a fresh blanket of snow on the higher mountains and the air was so smooth it was as if we were riding on a magic carpet. As we slowly climbed up the valley, the rugged mountains were just off each wingtip until we flew so low over the pass that you could see sparkles off the fresh snow crystals. I gently pulled the power back and we began a slow decent over Puget Sound towards SeaTac Airport. As the passengers disembarked they all commented on the beautiful flight until the last passenger. He could hardly talk – he stammered and stuttered so bad I thought he was really scared and was trying to think of what I could say if he reported me to the FAA for flying so low. Finally, he spit it out and said, "It was so beautiful, it was a religious experience". Whew!

Our usual routing from Portland to Bellingham took us west of Seattle but if the weather was really nice, I'd cancel the instrument flight plan and head directly to Mount Saint Helens. We'd fly past the west side and then begin a turn to the right, so the passengers were looking directly into the side of the crater caused by the catastrophic 1980 eruption. As we came low around to the south rim, I'd pull the power back and we'd drop into the crater and fly out the north side. Occasionally passengers would complain because they didn't have time to get their cameras out, but most felt it was better than any E-ride they'd ever been on.

Beech 99 15-passenger turboprop

Life was good. Even though the pay wasn't great the flying was fun. We had bought a house with five-acres east of Bellingham that had a great view of Mount Baker, a big barn and an art studio for Rica. The airline had gotten Beechcraft 99 turboprops and Alaska Airlines signed a "letter of intent" to buy San Juan as their regional commuter airline but then the bubble burst. The "letter of intent" was just a ploy to bring Horizon Air back to the bargaining table and a deal was struck for them to become Alaska's commuter. This made San Juan's creditors nervous and I could see the handwriting on the wall, again!

When the doors closed at San Juan Airlines a blind ad appeared in the Bellingham ads for turboprop pilots. Obviously somebody knew that there were some unemployed pilots around Bellingham, but who? Naturally I sent a resume and was anxious to find out who that was. A week later the phone rang, and an unidentified man began asking about my experience. Finally, he asked me if I had any problem flying a Casa 212 (Spanish twin turboprop) low level over jungles at night. This sounded exciting but probably not without a bit of danger, which should have paid accordingly. When he said the salary was $30,000 a year I lost interest but not before first finding out it was Evergreen Helicopters. I later also found out that they do some clandestine work other than just fighting forest fires with helicopters, etc. and this job would have involved dropping supplies to Panamanian rebels trying to oust President Noriega.

CHAPTER 8
de HAVILLAND
"OTTERS"

In the late 1960's Les LeBar saw an opportunity. United Parcel Service (UPS) wanted to serve the San Juan Islands but didn't find it economical to have their own people scattered around an area with such little revenue. Les grew up in the Islands, had a plane and made UPS a proposal which they found acceptable. He contracted with them to pick up their parcels for the Islands at their distribution point in Burlington and distribute them in the Islands. At first he did most of it himself, but the Islanders soon discovered the convenience of having things delivered to their door, rather than having to take the ferry to the mainland for shopping, and his business grew.

We often chatted about the ideal plane for his particular operation. The Cessna 207 he was using then was getting too small and most bigger planes were twins and needed longer runways than the Islands had. There was one single engine plane made in Canada, that would fit the bill, but they were pretty expensive. Les finally bit the bullet and bought his first de Havilland DHC-3 "Otter". By the time San Juan Airlines closed its doors, Aeronautical Services had three partners, an operation in California serving Catalina Island and three Otters and a 207 and a need for another pilot.

Flying the Otter was a hoot, except in a crosswind. It had a 600 horsepower Pratt & Whitney "Wasp" radial engine on the front, a large cargo capability and was a taildragger with excellent short field performance. Starting these engines was a multi-step procedure that, if done incorrectly, could damage the engine. First you made sure that the magnetos were turned off, then manually pulled the engine through nine compression strokes to make sure there was no hydraulic lock in a cylinder, then back in the cockpit to engage the starter switch which spun up the inertial starter, then engage the inertial starter clutch with another switch which caused the engine to turn over, then turn on the fuel pump, then begin to pump the throttle and then turn on the magnetos. The result of all this was a lot of smoke, shaking, backfiring and other noises especially on cold winter mornings and sometimes even a fire which meant using the fire extinguisher to put out a carburetor fire and then starting the process all over again. Rather than mufflers the Otter had straight exhaust pipes which ran into four augmenter tubes which used exhaust pulses to help draw cooling air through the engine. They had quite a unique sound and pretty soon everyone in the Islands knew when the big blue UPS planes were coming. But, many people were genuinely surprised when they casually waved at an Otter flying by and the pilot would stick his arm out the window and wave back. Two of our Otters were ex-Canadian Army planes. One day an employee had to fly from Lopez to Friday Harbor with me and after she got buckled into the copilot's seat, jokingly picked up a tube under the instrument panel, put it to her lips and said, "Copilot to pilot, over." I asked if she knew what that tube was and she responded, "Intercom, right?" I said, "No, it's a relief tube."

As mentioned in Chapter 1, the first airplane ride of my life was from Long Beach to Catalina Island so when one of the partners, Steve Franklin, needed a vacation and wondered if I'd be interested in staying in his house and flying that route for a month I jumped at it. Rica and I visited family and old friends and I reminisced about that first flight there 38 years prior. A couple years later Steve had outgrown the Otter and bought two Douglas DC-3's and wondered if we'd be interested in moving back to Long Beach to fly them. What a nostalgic job that would have been, but we had left the Southern California rat race for a reason and that reason was still there.

The Otter engine produced a lot of heat and in the summer we often flew with the windows open. This caused me a big problem over the waters of Puget Sound one day when I took the flight manual and official documents for the plane out of the door pocket to look something up and the wind coming through the open window snatched them all right out of my hand and out the window. It was a real pain to replace the Airworthiness Certificate, official Flight Manual and Registration papers.

The R-1340 was the first engine designed by Pratt & Whitney and, in 1925, set new standards for performance and reliability but that was a long time ago and things have changed. Our mechanics did an admirable job of keeping these relics flying but "shit happens." Pratt & Whitney's logo says "Dependable Engines" but in 18,000 hours of flying, this is the only engine that has ever let me down — twice. Once, just after takeoff on Shaw Island's downhill runway -BANG-SHAKE-SHAKE-SHAKE! One-cylinder head broke off, but the engine kept running on the eight remaining cylinders long enough to get me back to Friday Harbor. Another time it quit at 800' over the water but I was able to glide to Lopez Island and land on a road.

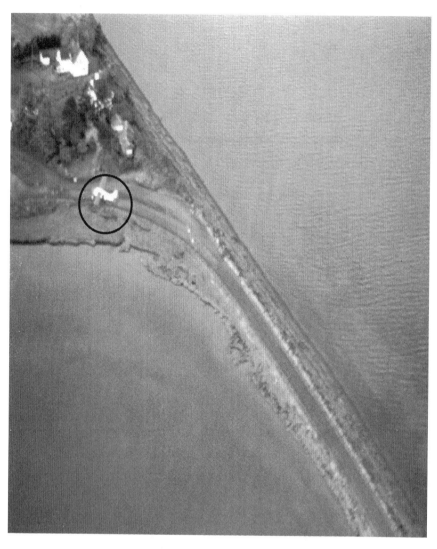

When the engine quits, land anywhere you can!

Flying for Aeronautical Services was a lot of fun. I had weekends off, was home every night and was often able

Co-pilot grandson Kern

to take friends along in the copilot's seat for some *real flying* but when a friend told me about some flying he had done in Africa ----.

CHAPTER 9
AIRSERV AFRICA

ETHIOPIA

AirServ International was a non-profit, humanitarian airlift company headquartered in Redlands, California (now Warrenton, Virginia) but whose main work was in the trouble spots of Africa. I applied and then began a few of the most challenging, rewarding and interesting years of our lives. After sending in my resume, Del Kirkpatrick, the director of human resources at AirServ and former pilot in Africa, invited us to Redlands for an interview. At the time their planes were mostly Cessna Caravans, de Havilland Twin Otters and a few Cessna piston engine planes based in Mozambique, Ethiopia, Kenya, Uganda and Sudan but they were often moved around, depending on where the need was. Most of their work was contracts with the United Nations or larger NGO's (Non-Government Organizations). They had their roots in the Mission Aviation Fellowship (MAF) but in 1984 separated to help on famine relief in drought-stricken Ethiopia. They also saw the need for safe, mobile, non-sectarian air transport in the Third World and it grew from there.

They say the way to a man's heart is through his stomach. The Seventh Day Adventist Church in Walla Walla put on a famine fund raising dinner featuring

Ethiopian food in 1985 and I was hooked. It's still one of my favorites. Nine years later I was offered a two-year contract with AirServ and we picked Ethiopia as our first choice of countries as our base. It worked and we would be living in Addis Ababa flying a Cessna Caravan. I gave notice at Aeronautical Services, we rented out our house and said our "goodbyes"

We arrived about 8 PM and were met by the Ethiopia program manager, Elwin Windsor and his wife Gloria, who took us to our new home. It was surrounded by a seven-foot wall and the gate in front was manned 24-hours by security guards, armed with a baseball bat. It was nicely furnished, had pastries and a loaded coffee maker in the kitchen, two bedrooms and an empty servants' quarters behind the house. There was also an older Peugeot car in the driveway. In the morning Gloria and Elwin came over to explain the ins and outs of life in Ethiopia and take us on a tour of the city. Boil and filter your water, disinfect or cook all food, be prepared for power outages, consider it a good day if a phone call actually goes through and don't give to beggars in public places or you will be besieged. The extremes in the city were glaring – some new high rises but many shacks with dirt floors and rusted tin roofs, plus beggars and poverty everywhere. Most of the streets were somewhat paved but had few lane markings and traffic wandered randomly. Large chuck holes probably gave a lot of work to suspension repair shops. We came across a body lying in the middle of the street and Elwin, seeing the shock on my face, warned us not to stop or we might somehow become implicated. We drove by the opulent Hilton Hotel and Elwin told us that we would have passes to use the pool and other facilities there which, at first, I didn't understand. It became apparent that our house was definitely upper middle class, even though the street in front was dirt and full of ruts.

Our house in Addis Ababa

AirServ was very safety conscious and had first rate aircraft maintenance. Company rules required that all pilots must have fifty hours experience in each type of airplane before they were able to fly alone so Elwin flew with me for the first few weeks – and that was actually a very good thing. Around Addis we used VHF radios for communication but further out, all communications were with long range HF radios. This is the kind that has all kinds of skips, jumps and static but was used to make our arrival, departure and thirty-minute position reports. Ethiopian air traffic controllers didn't have radar, weren't used to handling much traffic either and sometimes were pretty hard to deal with if there were two planes in the air at once. The Cessna Caravan was basically a single engine turboprop freighter designed for FedEx as a feeder airplane, but a 10-seat passenger version was also available. It was very reliable and even though designed for operating on paved runways, it does an admirable job as long as dirt runways are long and solid enough. The Pratt & Whitney PT-6 turboprop engine will run on almost anything that burns but occasionally the mechanics would complain when we had to use dirty diesel fuel rather than jet fuel because it meant a messy job of changing fuel filters.

Most of our flying was to the east and south, toward Somalia and Kenya and necessitated refueling from fifty-five-gallon drums placed at runways along the way. Here I use the word "runway" loosely. Even though we had GPS (which was just coming online) that showed the exact location of the "runway", some were still hard to spot from 1000' in the air, or even on the ground. They were roughly a somewhat straight line in the desert where some of the brush had been removed. After hand pumping one or two barrels of fuel into the plane in 110 degree heat it felt really good to climb back up to 10,000' and cooler air. The occasional flights westerly towards Sudan or north though the Rift Valley were a welcome change of scenery.

Life in Addis was working out good for us. Rica had planned to get involved in some kind of volunteer work while we were there, such as assisting at a crafts school, but her passport had a big stamp on it saying, "May not work, paid or unpaid." She did make friends at the US and Canadian Embassies and got involved in making blankets and such which were distributed to the needy. I usually took *matatus* (small local buses) if I could, to avoid driving through the frightful traffic or hassle of trying to find parking. When I came home from work one day, Rica proudly announced that she had driven to a friend's house on the other side of Addis which necessitated driving through *confusion corner,* a six-way intersection with no traffic control. I think there is a video of that intersection on You Tube – pretty scary.

We asked one of our guards where he would eat in our neighborhood if he were going out for a bite. He said the *kebele* and showed us the way. It was at one of the neighborhood social centers that were built during the previous Communist regime and was good and cheap. We especially liked the lentil and bean dishes that were served during lent when the devout Orthodox Christians didn't eat meat. The day before Easter, the biggest Holy Day of their year, no animals in Ethiopia were safe. Everyone was dragging a reluctant cow, sheep, goat or chicken home for the next day's feast. Since our neighborhood was rather upscale, for Ethiopia, some of our neighbors spoke English and we were beginning to make some friends in the area. One thing that I am a little embarrassed to admit though, is that seeing all the other poverty daily can become a little overwhelming. That's what the passes to the Hilton were for, an escape.

Our guard, Ambelu, trying to teach me Amharic

An NGO called Africare had an office below ours and I got to know the director there. He was originally from Tombstone, Texas but had married an Ethiopian and had teen-aged kids. Their NGO was developing water and irrigation systems in needy areas and when he found out that I'd been a surveyor in a previous life asked if I'd be interested in working with his engineer sometime. Asefa had just graduated from the university in civil engineering and was pretty sharp but didn't have much practical experience. They needed to run some elevation profiles for calculating pressures in a new water system they were developing. When I asked my boss, he was tickled to give me some time off so he could fly occasionally. This was really getting to be a dream job – working with and getting to know local people AND flying. Then the boom fell – our contract with the UN was ending and they decided to give it to a local company. In all honesty, that was quite justified, but we were just beginning to feel comfortable there and like we could make a small difference. The UN must have recognized our sadness and when we wanted to rent the airplane for a personal trip to Lalibela they gave us a wonderful gift. We were able to use the plane for a day free of charge and they arranged for a bus to take us from the airstrip to the village and provided us with a guide and lunch for the whole AirServ staff. Lalibela is a few hundred miles north of Addis and known for its twelve monolithic Coptic churches hewn out of solid rock between the 10th and 14th centuries (that's before dynamite and jackhammers, folks).

Losing that contract posed a bit of a problem for AirServ since we were only four months into our two-year contract. There was a need for a pilot at a UN camp in Lokichogio, Kenya but they didn't think it was appropriate for this old couple.

SUDAN
Ask anyone where Sudan is, and you'll probably get a blank stare. Sure, they've recently heard about a new country somewhere called South Sudan but that's about it. Sudan was conquered by Egypt in 1874 and they were

both taken over by Britain in 1898 and then gained independence in 1953. I won't attempt to explain how the borders were defined in this multi-ethnic and diverse geographic region but suffice to say, the borders laid out by Europe did nothing to promote peace and tranquility in the area. Sudan has the Nile River running south to north through it and borders the Red Sea on the northeast and has some oil reserves in middle.

LIFESTYLE

Northern Sudan is Arabic and largely desert but is the seat of the economic, political and military power of the country. Southern Sudan is a large, fertile savanna with the Sudd, the largest swamp in the world, in its center. The people there are various black tribes who are animist or Christian and are mostly subsistence farmers. A subsistence farmer is one who lives on what he raises and barters. Southern Sudan has no highways (as we know them) and the villages have no grocery stores.

THE CONFLICT

As one can imagine, an Islamic, Arab ruling class and a black Christian under-class is a recipe for unrest. Unfortunately, when the South is not fighting the North, they are fighting each other. Now picture this – a roving militia in the south, fighting for what *they* believe in, needs food and comes into a village demanding half of a farmer's harvest and maybe one or two of their teen-aged sons for their militia. This forced a migration of starving people to somewhere – anywhere, in hopes of finding food. Another related migration of 15,000 to 20,000 boys, later called the *Lost Boys of Sudan*, headed eastward in the late 80's and early 90's, on an epic journey towards Ethiopia and then on to Kenya hoping to avoid being conscripted into a militia. That is a story of hardship, sadness, tragedy and hope that I wish somebody would make into a feature length documentary.

THE RESULT

An attempt in 1989 by the UN to mitigate one of the largest humanitarian disasters of modern times was the formation of Operation Lifeline Sudan. A camp and an unlit but paved runway were built next to the small village of Lokichogio in the very northwest corner of Kenya, about 20-miles from the Sudan and Ugandan borders. Various NGO's also moved into the UN camp or established their own nearby and the Red Cross set up a hospital to treat war wounded that were flown in from the fighting. The UN setup temporary food distribution centers in south Sudan which became semi-permanent until the refugees could feel secure in returning to their home villages.

The government of Sudan viewed this as an attempt by the UN to support an independence movement of the southern Sudanese and attempted to bomb the camp by rolling bombs out the back of a transport plane. This was viewed as an act of war by Kenya and they were able to get some American Hawk anti-aircraft missile batteries to defend the camps. The UN then agreed to form Operation Lifeline Sudan – Northern Sector, with an office and plane in Khartoum and somewhat mollified the Sudanese government.

LOKI, June 1994

We boarded a DC-3 in Nairobi, Kenya and ended up at a place resembling the set of the old TV series M.A.S.H. It

Entrance to U.N. camp at Lokichogio, Kenya

was a conglomeration of wood and brick huts called *tukuls*, tents and old shipping containers. The camp had a chain link fence around it and a gate at the front with guards armed with AK-47's, not baseball bats. There was a mess tent with tables outside under the thorny acacia trees and an open wash area featuring pit toilets and cold showers. We got an eight-sided wooden hut with a thatched roof that was to become our home for most of the next one and a half years.

Our home for one-and-a-half years

Actually, it wasn't all that bad. You started out with a bed and based on seniority, whenever someone else left, the next most senior person got whatever furniture they wanted to make their life more comfortable – a closet, chest, table, mini refrigerator (for tonic and beer), radio, etc. The company even sent up a TV-VCR combo, popcorn maker and new movies every week. Saturday evening was BBQ night featuring local game animals and volleyball afterwards. One week the company sent the video *Cool Running* up and we invited our four African airport helpers to our tukul on a Saturday night for a movie and popcorn. Those guys had never seen snow before, just like the Jamaican bobsled team. What a riot, watching them watch the movie!

Every morning you left your dirty clothes on the floor; when you returned in the evening the washed and ironed clothes were neatly laid out on your bed. Often the ironed clothes had little burn holes in them from the charcoal heated irons. There were mandatory security briefings at 6 PM, then the bar opened (BYO) and a buffet style dinner featuring African and Western style food was served at 7 PM. After dinner you could return to the bar, but the pilots' breakfast was at 6 AM so we were usually in bed early. You could get bag lunches, but they weren't very good.

One day Knut, our Norwegian co-pilot took one bite of his sandwich and threw it out the window in disgust. Naturally, when the sandwich hit the 140 mph slipstream it came flying back through the window and hit Knut right in the middle of the face and then splattered it all over the cockpit, except a slice of tomato and onion which were stuck on his face. We couldn't help but laugh but he then had to clean up the mess in the cockpit. About 10 PM, the malaria-bearing mosquitoes came out. Thankfully, we had screens on our windows and took regular doses of chloroquine, an anti-malaria drug and never did get it. There were beautiful birds in the area and some people became avid bird watchers. If you were an entomologist, every month there was a different crop of bugs dropping down your back from the trees above. There was even something for herpetologists – Egyptian cobras, green mambas, ugly puff adders and the very deadly black mambas. There were usually about a hundred people, from everywhere in the world, in camp at any one time.

Typical village scene in South Sudan

Many of our flights from Loki were to villages in the Sudd (swamp) and by the time we were unloaded, the plane was full of flies that came off the sores on the natives who were helping us unload the Twin Otter. We carried a Kenyan bug spray called "Doom," but some pilots didn't feel comfortable inhaling that on a regular basis, so we came up with an ingenious idea. When the end of a one-inch plastic tube, about five feet long, was stuck out the pilot's vent window it created enough vacuum to suck out all the flies in the cockpit within a matter of minutes and provided entertainment for the non-flying pilot.

The UN hired a former Kenyan cop to be the local head of security around the camp. Unfortunately, he was a genuine asshole and beat and otherwise mistreated kids who would play or beg outside the camp. After dinner one night a few pilots were standing around talking when some bullets came flying by and we hit the dirt. Rica had already gone back to our tukul, so I crawled on my belly, like a snake, a few hundred yards to see if she was okay. When I crawled in the door, it was dark. I said, "Rica, are you here?" I was so relieved to hear her say, "Yes, I'm over here." I said, "Where?" She replied, "Under the bed." Apparently some local fathers didn't like the way the camp security guy was treating their kids and began shooting at his brick tukul from outside the fence. He got scared and came running out, in our direction! Then, as one former British SAS officer said, the "sympathetic fire" began. Everyone with an AK-47 joined in and I'm not sure what they were shooting at, but it was really exciting. Finally, a Kenyan Army Company came over and joined in the shooting and things began to quiet down. The shooting had lasted for 36 minutes according to one witness. No one was hit, but some tukuls had bullet holes in them and there were new tree branches laying on the ground. When a new AirServ pilot, who was waiting at the guesthouse in Nairobi to catch a flight to Loki, heard about the shooting, he decided to quit and go home.

One morning at Loki I wasn't flying so I said, "Rica, let's go for a walk outside the camp and see what the surroundings are like." I picked up an interesting piece of red obsidian and was just looking for other interesting things when we came upon some teenaged goat herders, carrying AK-47's which cost $60 in Kenya.

A little further on we saw a human skull and Rica had enough and firmly said, "Let's get out of here." I had to fly soon anyway but as we turned to head back to camp, we saw two more skeletons. At lunch Rica was telling some pilots what we had seen, and they wanted her to show them where they were. She didn't find the ones we had seen but saw six others.

"Cattle Raiding" is a popular sport, if you want to call it that, among tribes in East Africa. They sneak in, in the middle of the night, and try to steal another tribe's cattle. In the old days, if the raid was discovered a spear fight ensued and if a young warrior was wounded, the resulting scar was a badge of honor (if he didn't die). Nowadays, with AK-47's, the results of a cattle raid are much more tragic. The skeletons we found were most certainly from the Traposa tribe to the north because the local Turkanas would bring their own fallen warriors' home for a fitting burial.

Flight attendant Tiana from Bellingham

AirServ had an apartment in Nairobi for the use of anyone not on duty in Loki. There was a Russian AN-34 plane that had a UN contract to make daily flights hauling freight and passengers to and from Nairobi. The flight attendant on that plane, named Tiana, had an American accent and I asked where she was from. "Bellingham, Washington." Small world!

Our pilots were limited to flying 8-hours a day in the single engine Caravan and 10-hours on the two pilot

Twin Otter. We were limited to 80-hours a month but usually extended to 100. The pilots kept a running total on a white board in the office, but a new base manager thought it looked tacky and said he'd keep the monthly totals in a book at his desk. One day he found me and excitedly said, "Rich, we're in trouble." I was wondering what I did this time when he confessed that I had already flown 140 hours that month, far over the legal limit. He had taken on the responsibility of watching our hours, but I guess he was able to straighten the error out. Our normal schedule usually had us flying for about 3 weeks and then a week off in Nairobi or wherever. We used the time off to go on safari, go to the coast, national parks, interior jungles, Zanzibar and even Greece.

Rica's office at Loki

Many friends ask Rica what she did in camp while I was out flying. She kept quite busy volunteering for UNICEF, taking minutes and notes at meetings and teaching a Kenyan girl she had befriended how to use a computer. She eventually got a good job with the Red Cross, which made Rica very happy that she could help a local get ahead. Once she taught the cooks at the mess hall how to make carrot cake. Naturally she had made many friends around the camp and when the logistician at OXFAM quit, she was hired for about three-months until they found a local replacement who she could train to take over her job.

She made daily contact on an HF radio with all their aid workers scattered around south Sudan and forwarded their needs to an office in Nairobi. When those supplies came into Loki, she arranged for getting them forwarded out to their aid workers in the field.

The flying was interesting. The Northwest, where I had done most of my flying, has few thunderstorms and they were isolated and interesting to fly around. South Sudan has a weather phenomenon known as *squall lines* during the rainy season in August. These can stretch for a hundred miles in each direction and are embedded with severe thunderstorms. Pilots flying in the American southeast are familiar with squall lines and treat them with great respect. Our planes had radar and on my first encounter with a squall line I figured we'd just find a thin spot on the radar and punch right on through. Holy shit!!! It turned us every way but loose. With the power at idle we were climbing 3000' per minute one second and then descending 3000' per minute at full climb power. I thought we would surely rip the wings off the Twin Otter. There was hail and lightening and turbulence like I had never imagined. It is said that flying is hours of sheer boredom punctuated by moments of stark terror; this was one of those moments. All you can do is fly the airplane, analyze the situation, sort out your options and try to pick the best one. Fortunately, our freight was well secured, and we had no passengers aboard. My plan to get through the squall line was okay but my understanding of the radar was not. What I had interpreted as the thinnest part of the *squall line* was actually the worst. It was so bad that the full extent of the thunderstorm was *attenuated* by the extremely heavy precipitation. Experience – a series of non-fatal mistakes or "Kraap, I'll never, **ever,** do that again."

Most of the strips were dirt, but fairly well marked. We had hand drawn sketches of each strip which we called our "Jungle Jepps." In airplane talk a "Jepp" is a map or chart made by Jeppesen Sanderson, Inc. that is used by most instrument pilots around the world. Ours showed the runway length, width, elevation, co-ordinates, surface, obstacles and nearby wrecks, trees and villages. Since our Twin Otter was the best short field airplane at Loki, when a new strip was opened we were the first plane in and drew a Jungle Jepp. It was also a chance to see the locals in their natural setting. The men wore a string around their waist and the women wore a little flap of leather over their groin area. Within a few weeks we flew in large bales of cloths, often from the Mormon Church of the United States "to clothe the naked." They were cut open and a free for all ensued. Of course, these people had little concept of the gender of these clothes, but the funniest sight was seeing a big Dinka warrior a few weeks later wearing a pink ballerina tutu he must have found attractive.

Arriving and departing Loki, we had to fly a route over specific check points, lest we supposedly would get shot down by the Hawk missile batteries. The guys at the missile sites seemed rather bored so we began honking our horn at them as we flew over and they seemed quite amused and waved back. They began waving as soon as they saw "UN Charlie Two" or "UN Forklift Ten", the call signs of our Cessna and Twin-Otter.

There was an odd assortment of other planes based at Loki. Two other operators were operating Caravans. It's a very reliable machine but it's no bush plane, although one operator was running it that way. If you constantly push things to the limit, it's only a matter of time before you get bit. They were trying to take a load out of a runway we refused to take our Caravan into and hit a soft spot on the runway on takeoff. The result was that they were going too fast to stop by the end of the runway, and too slow to get airborne and hit a crowd of people standing at the end of the runway. Eight dead and many more injured but the pilot still managed to coax the disabled plane into the air.

Another group of old men bid on hauling freight into south Sudan with two old DC-6's and a DC-7. I asked them how in the heck they could get in and out of some of those short strips, but one old codger explained that getting them stopped on the soft runways wasn't a problem and when they took off they were very light. The DC-7 crashed first. Then they began cannibalizing one of the Sixes to keep the other one running. Then it just disappeared. The Red Cross had a Twin Otter and a Turbine DC-3 that was operated by Zimex, a Swiss company and they ran their operation like, well, a Swiss watch. Someone else ran a piston engine DC-3 out of Loki for a while and we passed them on the way into south Sudan once and noticed the back door was opened. We called and asked if it was for ventilation, but they said it was to make it easier to jettison load if they lost an engine.

Many of the operators were paid by the pounds they hauled so consequently they flew overloaded. A C-46 lost an engine after takeoff and just barely managed to keep out of the bush for a couple miles trying to get back to the runway until the pilot finally gave up and pulled the power back on the good engine and bellied it in. They salvaged the radios and instruments and just left the rest out in the bush. There were also two big de Havilland Buffaloes operating out of Loki which should have been great bush planes – they packed a large load out of short runways, but they were expensive to keep running and had weak nose gears. Both planes were down at once for a while with collapsed nose wheels.

Since South Sudan was a war zone our flying was mostly done above 10,000', to be out of range of small arms fire. This was fine with us since it was cooler up there but in the back some of our African passengers would be shivering and looking for something to cover up with. Some flights involved evacuating NGO's in danger or war wounded. Though the nearby Red Cross hospital was primarily for treating wounded, we would occasionally bring them other injured such as snake bite victims and on three occasions, victims of hyena attacks. With some, gangrene had set in and the smell coming into the cockpit was enough to make one vomit, forcing us to shut the door to the cabin. The strips we flew into had to be declared safe before we would fly in; still one of our planes hit a land mine and was damaged so they ran cows on the strip for six months before we would return. The cows missed one, but we found it. It was the same co-pilot on both of those flights, and he quit shortly thereafter.

We had some known safe areas stored in our GPS's and on return flights, when we were often empty, we would fly low and look at wildlife. What a treat viewing the thousands of migrating antelopes, zebras, wildebeests and other, fewer, elephants, lions, hippos, giraffes, etc. When we arrived at a village we first made a low pass (15') over the runway, blasting the horn, to get the animals and people off the runway. Didn't always work – hit a crocodile once that crossed the runway just as we touched down. Thunk! After unloading we taxied back, and it was gone – don't know if he wasn't badly hurt or some natives had him for dinner. Once, after taking off from a village, Knut was in a left turn back towards Loki when we were confronted with a large flock of birds spiraling upward up in a thermal. It happened so fast he could take no evasive action and a large Marabou stork came right by my side of the plane and hit something, maybe the landing gear. We were lucky, they can take out windshields or engines but good old Forklift Ten just kept cruising as if nothing had happened. Back at Loki I was looking for damage around the left landing gear when a mechanic inquired as to what was wrong. I told him we'd hit a big bird and he began looking. "There it is," he said pointing up to a dent in the upper side of the vertical stabilizer. Apparently it had ricocheted off the tire and hit up there.

An operation named Southern Air Transport (SAT) operated a C-130 Hercules out of Loki, mostly doing air drops. A wild bunch, they also did work for the CIA or anyone with cash. We could fly along as observer's which was fun. The floor of the C-130 was covered with rollers and when they reached the drop zone at 800' the captain would pitch the nose of the plane up and tell the load master when to release the load. Seventeen tons would roll out the back in about three seconds. When that load hit the ground, the vibration was pretty impressive.

C-130 doing airdrops of sorghum

Coming back to Loki after their last run of the day, the 4th of July, this big four engine transport buzzed the camp about 50' over the treetops to let everyone know they were hosting a big party at their camp that night. The camp manager was livid and at the security briefing that night announced that if anyone ever did that again, they would never fly for the UN again. Not to be intimidated by that little Yugoslavian guy, after breakfast the next morning they did it again. Within a week the Belgian Air Force had a C-130 at Loki and SAT was gone. The Russians operating the daily shuttle to Nairobi were feeling frisky one day and buzzed the control tower. They, too, lost their contract.

KHARTOUM

The base manager called me into his office. "Rich, how would you and Rica like to go to Khartoum for a month?" AirServ had a Twin Otter based there but the UN decided a smaller Caravan would do the job. The problem was that our rules said that pilot must have 50 hours in that type of plane before they could fly it solo. Kurt Neuenschwander had a lot of experience but still had to have someone fly with him for that first 50 hours in a new plane. What a great opportunity for us to see another part of Africa. Rica and I picked up a Caravan in Entebbe, Uganda and flew it to the capitol of the Islamic Republic of Sudan and moved into the same apartment building as Kurt, Angie and their family.

As I entered flight time in my logbook I noticed – 15,000 hours. Where had the time gone; seemed like yesterday that I was yearning for that first thousand hours or two and now the hours just keep rolling in, but no jet time, though we were having fun. Our job there was to fly NGO and UN personnel and supplies south from Khartoum to various locations supported by Operation Lifeline Sudan – Northern Sector. Khartoum is at the confluence of the Blue Nile coming from Ethiopia and the White Nile coming north from the Sudd Swamp in South Sudan. The city seems dirty as is to be expected, surrounded by desert and besieged by dust storms called *haboobs.*

There is an irrigated agricultural area south of Khartoum between the Blue and White Niles that resembles Imperial Valley in California in that it is a large blotch of vivid green surrounded by brown desert. When the irrigation potential of this area was discovered and water began being pumped out of the rivers, Egypt, to the north began to notice a lower flow of vital water coming into their country and threatened war. In 1929 an agreement was reached that four-billion cubic meters of water must be allowed to flow across the border into Egypt annually. Engineers in Egypt back in the 1920's already had a brilliant idea for getting more water to irrigated areas downstream. Coming north through the Sudd Swamp the Blue Nile lost half of its water due to evaporation, transpiration and percolation but if the swamp could be bypassed with a canal, that water could be used for agriculture up north. Unfortunately, they didn't give any thought to the cultural and environmental damage such an endeavor would cause to the people and wildlife around the swamp. The largest, at that time, self-propelled land machine in the world began digging a canal at Malakal in 1978 and headed in almost a straight line towards Bor, 224 miles to the south. The *Jonglei Canal* made it 149 miles before war and environmental concerns halted the project in 1983 and the huge, rusting excavator still sits in the canal where the project was halted. We often crossed it on our way to destinations in south Sudan.

Khartoum leaves one with mixed impressions. At our entrance to the airport, there were always about eight to ten guys sitting around not doing much. Kurt said they all belonged to different government security agencies and their job was to watch *each other* as well as the people coming into the airport.

 The city had a large drainage system to route off water in event of the infrequent rainstorms. These concrete drainage canals alongside the streets were about five feet deep and covered with rectangular, perforated concrete lids that also served as sidewalks. Great idea but occasionally one would get broken or damaged by a heavy truck or whatever and never replaced, making walking on the sidewalks at night quite hazardous.

One Friday we went to Omdurman, across the Nile from Khartoum, to watch the Whirling Dervishes and do some sightseeing. The Dervishes are an offshoot of Islam noted for their dances where they twirl and spin till they fall to the ground in exhaustion or a trance. We also went to an area with a wide riverbank to watch them building river boats and firing bricks.

As we were leaving some people in a nearby building waved at us to come over. Somewhat reluctantly, we did and were given a very impromptu but interesting tour of a pottery where they made large water jugs that stood on racks around the city, the equivalent of our drinking fountains. The jugs were unglazed so as water seeped through the porous pot and evaporated, it cooled the water within. People used a tin can to scoop out the cool drinking water. The potter used a large old-fashioned kick wheel and the jugs were so tall they had to be made in three lifts and then fired in a large wood fired kiln. Rica found this interesting, as she had an electric wheel and kiln at her studio back in the United States.

Grocery shopping was usually done in large, mostly open-air market areas. When Rica bought meat in the market she pointed to the section of the lamb or cow she wanted (no pork) and the butcher would cut off a chunk. It was all the same price – filet minion or chuck roast.

The UN paid for using our plane a minimum of sixty-hours a month. That month they hadn't used the plane for the minimum and would lose that time, so they decided to fly to the pyramids at Meroe, about 125 miles north of Khartoum. Kurt and I could bring our wives along. The pyramids were the tombs of the kings and queens in the ancient kingdom of Kush. We landed at a little dirt airstrip about three miles from the pyramids and walked to the tombs in the blazing heat.

Pyramids at Meroe

After touring the tombs, Kurt and I wondered why we didn't just land in the desert next to the tombs rather than walking all that way. We went back and got the plane and flew back to pick up our passengers at the pyramids. While we went to get the plane, people, camels and donkeys showed up and they began selling stuff – knives, clothes, jewelry, camel rides, etc. This was in the Sahara Desert – we had no idea where they came from! The day turned out to be quite an unexpected treat.

Rica left for Loki a few days before me. The last evening in Khartoum I needed a little fruit for breakfast in the next morning and stopped at a little roadside fruit stand. The owner certainly wouldn't have spoken English, so I just smiled at him and babbled something about him having the best fruit in Sudan, blah, blah...while I picked out a grapefruit, orange and banana. Then I handed him some money, expecting him to take what he needed but he said, "You can have it. You're my friend." in very good English. I felt so overcome by this gesture of friendship to a total stranger from America that it brought tears to my eyes. The US has demonized Sudan, but remember, *the people* are not the government or the powerful religious fundamentalists.

BACK AT LOKI

The sojourn to Khartoum was interesting but Loki also had its interesting moments. A renegade militia in south Sudan with northern sympathies raided the village of Waat and took eleven NGO workers and their vehicles as hostages and headed north. The UN dispatched our two AirServ planes to search for them and the observer in my plane did spot them driving north through the bush. I circled and dropped a little lower to get a better look but

Hostages rescued from southern Sudanese militia

the security chief riding with us warned, "They have machine guns!" so we climbed back up to a safer altitude. It took a few days of negotiations before we got them back. The Loki runway wasn't lighted so when we returned with the hostages on the third night, the runway was lit with coffee cans filled with burning diesel fuel. The next night we had one of the most joyous parties I've ever attended and the whole camp turned out to hear the individual hostage's stories.

For a few years the Kenyan government had been demanding that AirServ register our US registered airplanes with them and that we pilots and mechanics should get Kenyan licenses. This would have presented major problems since we moved equipment and personnel around to different countries so often. Finally, AirServ said that we should at least go through the motions of complying and we began studying for the Kenyan pilots written test. After taking the test I checked on a few questions that I wasn't sure of, but my answers were correct, so I guessed that my score would be in the high 90%'s. After a few weeks I got a postcard that merely said "failed". I was livid! Talking to some pilots from other operators they were puzzled but then asked, "You paid them off, didn't you?" They had paid off the right people and got their licenses without taking any tests, flight or written.

GIVING AID
Reflecting on our time in Africa, a few things regarding aid became apparent. It must be conditional, it must be

temporary, and it must be appropriate.

- By conditional, the aid must include the people's participation in the project, such as building hospitals, schools, runways, etc.
- By temporary, the aid must help the people become self-sufficient as someday it will come to an end.
- By appropriate, the aid must reflect an understanding of local cultures, conditions and technologies which can be totally foreign to us.

I talked to some engineers who had been building dams in Somalia. The migratory goat herders in the area would stop at a watering hole until it ran dry and then move on again in search of water. This same drill had probably been going on for hundreds of generations but was not very conducive to a lifestyle which includes education, health care and a modern economy. Climate change was also causing more frequent droughts and famine. The plan was simple. They studied the percolation rate of the soil, the evaporation rate in the area, the drainage basin and runoff and built dams in some of the bigger wadis (seasonally dry riverbeds) so water would be available most of the year. Unfortunately, this caused overgrazing of the surrounding area and conflicts between different tribes wanting the better watering holes. The NGO's then had to go back and lower the dams somewhat so the watering holes would go dry occasionally, forcing the tribes to move on. The problem has no immediate, simple answer but we, the developed world, want to do something to help our suffering, fellow humans — but what?

A village we flew into in southeast Ethiopia had a polluted river about a mile from the village. Men with a string of donkeys filled up water jugs at the river and sold them in the village. A group of volunteers from Doctors Without Borders (MSF) put in a deep well near the river and a pipeline to a water point in the center of the village with clean water. It didn't take long before the waterline was ripped up by the now unemployed donkey drivers. This turmoil then resulted in a horrible cholera epidemic in the village. At that point MSF figured out that the best option was to put a tank at the well and let the donkey drivers go back to work hauling CLEAN water to the village. In retrospect, it's all so obvious!

I often traded t-shirts or bags of salt for spears and other souvenirs

OUT OF AFRICA

It was turning out to be near the end of our time in Kenya anyway, so getting Kenyan licenses wasn't an issue, but we had another problem. The program manager, when we arrived in Kenya, didn't want to go through the hoops of getting me a work permit and since we were in and out of Kenya so often, we just got 90-day tourist visas every three months. About a month before we were to leave, an immigration officer noticed all the tourist visa stamps in my passport and asked if I had been working in Kenya. I nervously said that I was working for the UN whereby he asked if I was an employee of the UN? I deferred to AirServ, who deferred to the UN, who did what they could. But Kenya was flexing their sovereignty and virtually put Rica and me under house arrest. We had one last trip planned, to Lamu, but were told we couldn't leave Nairobi until this was settled and that we could be facing jail time. This wasn't a pleasant ending to our almost two years in Africa, but we were finally released. And overall, we wouldn't have traded the experience for anything in the world.

On the way home in December 1995 we stopped in India for seven weeks and met our new son-in-law's family and really enjoyed seeing that interesting country. Upon arriving home our house was still rented out for four months. We got our old restored MGB out of the barn, loaded up a tent and sleeping bags (had to leave the spare tire) and drove to Southern California, across to Key West, up to Maine and finally home again. We visited many friends along the way and saw a lot of the US, but it was now time to settle down again and look for a job.

CHAPTER 10
CIRPAS

While I was doing some long-neglected chores around the house the phone rang. The voice introduced himself as Frank Scarabino, a former AirServ pilot who had also flown in Africa. He had called AirServ to see if they could recommend any former pilots who were now back in the States and might be looking for a job and my name came up. He was the chief pilot for a company called CIRPAS, based near Monterey, California and they were engaged in atmospheric research. "Interesting. What kind of plane do you use?" "Well" he said, "it's a bit of an odd duck that we call a Pelican". "Huh?"

Highly modified Cessna O-2 "Fighting Skymaster"

He went on to explain that it was a used Air Force O-2 Fighting Skymaster, which was the military equivalent of the civilian Cessna 337 Super Skymaster. They had been used in Vietnam as observation planes by forward air controllers. It was an unusual plane too, in that it's two engines were mounted in tandem on the front and back of the fuselage with twin booms going back to the tail. Because of its unusual appearance it had many nick names such as "huff 'n puff", "Mixmaster" and "push n' pull" but its unusual appearance didn't end there. CIRPAS had modified it by taking the 210-horsepower engine off the front and putting a long bulbous nose in its place to house scientific instruments. Of course, with half of its original 420 horsepower removed, it would

There used to be an engine here!

not have gotten off the ground, so they put a little bigger 300 horsepower engine on the rear – for a total loss of

120 of its original horsepower. Hmmm! It also had instrument pods, which resembled bombs, hanging on the wings and a long probe, resembling a 50-caliber gun sticking out the nose. It's maximum endurance aloft was 24 hours (far beyond that of any ordinary pilot) and a leisurely cruise speed of 90 knots and supposed max altitude of 12,000 feet. I just had to see this thing, so I took the job. Frank said that he didn't know how long I'd be needed – it just depended on what other research projects came in, but they had two scheduled at the moment, one in the Canary Islands and one in Southern California.

CIRPAS is owned by the US Naval Post Graduate School in Monterey, California. Our paychecks came from Cal Tech and we had instruments aboard the airplane from NASA, University of Washington, NOAA, Princeton, Cal Berkeley, Office of Naval Research, Cal Tech and others. The first month in Monterey I helped prepare the plane for its flight to Tenerife in the Canary Islands, went through the Navy's sea survival schools at Patuxent, Maryland and Lemoore, California, did familiarization flights on the Pelican and arranged transportation for all the associated equipment we'd need on the project. While training with a bunch of F-18 supersonic fighter pilots at Lemoore Naval Station I could see that they were a little curious about the old, gray bearded guy in their midst until one finally asked. When I explained that the O-2 we were flying belonged to the Naval Postgraduate School, was loaded with scientific gear and had one engine removed, they just gasped and shook their heads. ACE-2 was a large collaborative atmospheric research project that included ground stations in Portugal, Madeira and Tenerife, a Russian ship, a big four engine British C-130 turboprop, a Dutch Swearingen turboprop, a German Dornier 228 turboprop, a French Falcon jet, various NASA and NOAA satellites and the US representative, our small piston engine airplane. Frank and his co-pilot Dave flew the Pelican across the US, the North Atlantic and down to the Canary Islands, off the coast of Africa and we began three months of most interesting work.

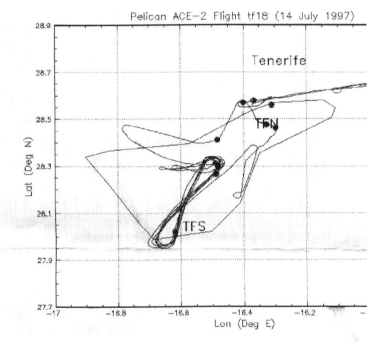

Patterns flown doing atmospheric research

The team consisted of a mechanic, about 25 scientists, a few other support people and four pilots, Frank, Dave, myself and Carlos, a local Spanish pilot who would be my co-pilot. Actually, another local named Jose was scheduled to be my co-pilot but the day before we were supposed to start flying he was out with a student pilot and they crashed, killing both of them. It was quite a shock. We kept the Pelican at the Tenerife Flying Club where both Carlos and Jose were young flight instructors trying to build time and everybody knew everybody. At Jose's funeral there were so many people that I couldn't even get inside the church.

This drawing hung above the bar at the Pelican Club

At the airport bar, the other pilots often bought us drinks and offered us sympathy for the funny little plane we had to fly but did accept us and the Pelican as part of the ACE-2 team and the flying club. In fact, after a few weeks they renamed the bar at the airport the Pelican Club. We did most of the low-level work while the jet and turboprops did the higher-level work. Most days we were up for six to eight hours but one day Frank and Dave got a flight that I was glad someone else had to do. They flew at exactly 8000' for twelve hours, turning left three degrees every minute! The patterns we flew varied from day to day. Some days we rendezvoused with the other planes at different altitudes to sample the particulates in an air mass coming down from Europe, sometimes we had to be at a specific location just as a satellite passed over to compare our light wave measurements with theirs or fly a large lazy eight pattern from afternoon till after sunset. Often I'd ask the scientists that had experiments on the plane that day what the objective was, and they all were too eager to talk about their projects but quickly lost me with their highly technical explanations. It was still interesting though. One flight we had to rendezvous with a Russian ship off the Moroccan coast, but they couldn't use their radios for the last two hours before we got there, so their coordinates were a little stale and we couldn't find them – a 600' ship! Carlos made an interesting comment. If we can't find a 600' ship and we ever had to ditch at sea, how could they ever find our little heads bobbing around in the water?

We always alternated flying to the project site and back but when we were on location Carlos handled the radios and computers, which were in front of him, and I did the pattern flying. As some of the places where we had to fly patterns took a few hours to get to, Carlos and I had lots of time to talk. I really enjoyed getting to know the

Spanish culture through him and the wonderful people who adopted us at the Aero Club; they took us all in like long-lost friends.

Rica also flew over for a few weeks. We had a great suite with a kitchen in a beautiful, large hotel overlooking the Atlantic Ocean. One evening Rica and I were sitting on the balcony watching the sunset and I said, "Look, there it is!" but she had just turned to look at a dog running across the lawn and missed it. "Missed what?" she asked. "The GREEN FLASH" I exclaimed. She looked at me kind of funny and thought maybe I'd better get to bed and get some rest. It really does exist — honest! Naturally, it was hard to leave that and our newfound friends, but we had to get back to California for the next project. I was hoping to fly back with Frank in the Pelican but when CIRPAS found out that two one-way tickets on the airlines would cost more than one round trip, I had to go back commercial and Dave went back over the Atlantic in the Pelican with Frank. Bummer! Flying across the North Atlantic would have been really interesting.

Having worked as a surveyor for the California Highway Department back in the early 1960's, I was very familiar with the smog in the Los Angeles basin, especially in the late summer. After refitting the Pelican in Monterey, it was flown to El Monte, just outside Los Angeles, to study the smog. What a disappointment that turned out to be for the team. By the late 1960's they had figured out that smog was unhealthy, and we'd better do something about it. California led and the Federal government followed by requiring auto manufacturers to begin cleaning up auto emissions and the results of our "sniffing" showed that the government regulations had worked.

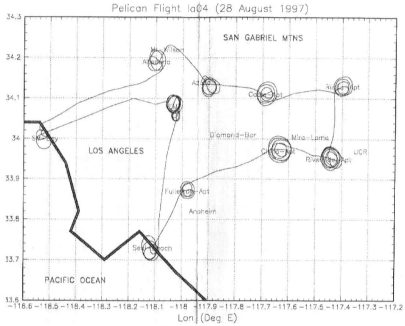

Patterns flown in Los Angeles basin

We flew from one end of the Los Angeles basin to the other, spiraling up or down in racetrack patterns between ground level to 12'000 feet and the results were generally astonishingly low. Dave was my co-pilot on this exercise. He had been a Marine pilot, had run a Marine survival school and then did a lot of relief work in Africa before running a river rafting business in Oregon, obviously a real tough guy but in reality a very mild mannered Mr. Nice Guy – not at all as his background might suggest. One thing you wouldn't have expected from this guy was a weak stomach. The scientists had picked up some interesting particulates in the eastern LA Basin that they wanted to study a little more, so one day Dave and I had to fly from San Bernardino to Garden Grove at low level, directly over the Freeway 91. Unfortunately, it was a very hot and turbulent day and we were really getting slammed around. Part way along the assigned route a terrible stench became almost overwhelming in the plane. Dave already had his face in a sic-sac but this smell was different – kind of a farm smell. Periodically I had to ask Dave to get his face out of the sic-sac long enough to reset a computer or change filters that were being used by some of the experiments. All in all, it was a rather miserable few hours for both of us but as we were finally taxiing back in at El Monte Dave took his face out of the barf bag, looked at me with tears streaming down his face and dried vomit on his chin and said, "It's not easy being a wimp." Turns out that the smell was in the area around Chino, which has a very large concentration of dairy farms. We now know that bovine flatulence is a significant source of methane, a strong greenhouse gas and it sure stinks, even at a thousand feet in the air.

When we returned the plane to Monterey in September, they didn't have any other flying coming up, so I went back to Bellingham – until the phone rang again.

CHAPTER 11
AIRSERV - UGANDA & BURUNDI

ENTEBBE

After two days of waiting in airports and three nights of flying I arrived in Uganda. Most of the serious aircraft maintenance work in Africa was being done in South Africa. AirServ saw an opportunity to establish a quality, for profit, repair facility and charter operation in central Africa and use the profits to subsidize its humanitarian work. AirServ Limited was formed and construction on a large hanger was begun in Entebbe, Uganda. I was needed for a few months until they got a permanent pilot there to fly charters. Most of the flying was for NGO's going to the troubled northern areas of Uganda.

The airport at Entebbe is noteworthy as the place where Israeli Commandos rescued 102 Jewish hostages taken on an Air France flight out of Tel Aviv. Remnants of that daring raid in July 1976 are still apparent at the airport, such as the bullet marks on the old terminal building and shot up Ugandan MIG-17 and MIG-21 fighter jets, now overgrown with weeds.

Shot-up MIG-17 and Entebbe airport terminal where Israeli hostage rescue took place

Uganda is a beautiful, lush green country but not without its problems. Remnants of the Lord's Resistance Army (LRA) still linger in the north and though the government is actively fighting corruption and lawlessness, some still exists. AirServ had rented three houses in a nice neighborhood one block from Lake Victoria. Late one night shortly before I arrived, an armed gang came ashore in a speedboat and broke into our mechanic's house, robbed the family, then shot and seriously wounded the mechanic. When I wasn't flying and had nothing else to do, I constructed two 15' tall steel towers for security lighting at the houses. Also, I had a little time for sightseeing at Bujagali Falls, where the Nile River exits Lake Victoria. They don't exist anymore since a new dam was constructed in 2011 and the falls were inundated. Occasionally I took local buses to go shopping or exploring in the nearby capital of Kampala.

Bujagali Falls

BURUNDI

Burundi is a small French speaking country with beautiful dense forest covered mountains, but it still has the same ethnic problems between the Hutu's and Tutsi's as neighboring Rwanda had. Such a pity. AirServ had a small

Twin Otter operation in Burundi and one of the pilots needed a break so I was going to go down to fill in for a couple weeks. This was just after the horrible genocide in Rwanda, but there was, and still is, unrest in that whole region. Fortunately, Dale Rose, the base manager, wasn't home one day when a bomb went off on a road and blew all the windows out of one side his house. He is also one of our pilots who had hit a land mine in Sudan.

A week before I was to leave, the news came that our Twin Otter had been shot up during a raid at the airport. The NGO's that we had been supporting throughout that country were now stranded. Finally, AirServ was able to break its Caravan in Entebbe loose and I flew it down to the capital of Bujumbura for two weeks so they could get things sorted out till we could get the Twin-Otter repaired or replaced.

The normal sequence of communications for a flight in most parts of the world run something like this:

> Bujumbura Clearance Delivery, this is UN Charlie 2 for clearance to Ruyigi.
> UN Charlie 2 you are cleared to Ruyigi as filed. Contact ground when ready for taxi
> Bujumbura Ground, UN Charlie 2 ready for taxi
> UN Charlie 2 taxi to runway 21, contact tower on 123.4 when ready for takeoff
> Bujumbura Tower, UN Charlie 2 ready for takeoff
> UN Charlie 2 cleared for takeoff. Contact Departure Control on 124.7 through 4
> Roger, good day, Charlie 2
> Bujumbura Departure, UN Charlie 2 through 4

UN Charlie 2, contact Burundi Center on HF 1234
Roger, Charlie 2
Burundi Center, UN Charlie 2 through 6 for 9.5
Roger UN Charlie 2, report position every 30
minutes and on ground at Ruyigi
Roger, Charlie 2
Burundi Center, UN Charlie 2 on ground at Ruyigi
Roger UN Charlie 2, report when ready to depart
Ruyigi

The humorous thing about this whole exchange of communications in Burundi was that it was the same voice on each frequency, and rarely did I hear another airplane on any frequency. One air traffic controller for a whole country!

On Sunday mornings the Soviet Embassy opened its grounds and people from all over met to play soccer and volleyball. In the afternoon we all went to a house that sold beer and enjoyed the camaraderie of people who didn't care about your ethnicity or nationality. I was talking to a local machinist who AirServ used to fabricate things they needed at the airport. He was one of those super nice and talented guys in his late 20's that could make most everything out of metal. As the evening and beers progressed, we began talking about families; he mentioned his mother was Tutsi and his father was Hutu and because of that neither side of his family accepted him. I was overcome by sadness and anger. This was a young man that anyone would be proud to call their son. Why in the hell can't people put aside their prejudices and just get along?

CHAPTER 12
AIRSERV - IRIAN JAYA

A severe *el Niño* in 1998 resulted in an unprecedented drought in the mountains of central New Guinea. Areas used to getting 200 inches of rain a year went for 5 months without a drop and the people living there normally raised three sweet potato crops a year as their primary staple crop. As the area faced massive starvation, the Red Cross, the Australian Government, the Mission Aviation Fellowship (MAF) and AirServ stepped up to help. Irian Jaya (now known as Irian Papua) is

the western half of the Island of New Guinea and belongs to Indonesia whereas the eastern half is the independent country of Papua New Guinea.

We were just getting ready to build a new house at Lake Samish when AirServ called but I agreed to go down there for four months. It was probably the most interesting, rewarding and challenging four-months of my life. AirServ deemed the Twin Otter as the best plane to haul reasonable loads into the rugged terrain and leased one in the Philippines. I replaced one of the pilots already down there and began learning the ropes.

Many of the landing strips (shown above) were on hillsides or steep valleys and once the approach was begun, you were committed to landing. The MAF pilots had their own version of the "Jungle Jepps" we used in Africa and they were a great help. They showed features around the strips and had a "final point" such as a hut or river crossing which should be crossed at a specific altitude and airspeed from which you set the power for a stabilized approach to the bottom end of the runway. Most of the strips were at between 4 and 9 thousand feet elevation (MSL) and some of the surrounding mountains went up to 16,000 feet. After touching down you needed to add power to get to the top of the strip where you could turn around and unload. If you didn't add power soon enough and the plane stopped on the hillside it would have flopped back on its tail and damaged the plane.

One morning we were landing into the sun and a shadow from the mountain was covering the upper half of the strip. After passing the "final point" it appeared almost like something was in the shadows on the runway. The copilot and I strained our eyes to figure out what we were looking at when three camouflage helicopters suddenly became apparent. Full power and a gentle right turn into rising terrain with a heavy load brought the pucker factor up to a 9.5 on a scale of 10. I really thought we'd take some branches off the treetops before we completed the turn back down the valley. They were Australian choppers unloading on the runway. We called AirServ on the HF radio and they gave us another village to drop our load at.

An even bigger challenge to flying in Irian Jaya was the weather. By six in the morning the weather was usually good enough to begin flying but by noon clouds began forming in the valleys and by 2 PM we often had to quit flying. We managed to get into one village at 3 PM but before we could get unloaded fog moved in and we spent the night in a missionaries' house.

Tough approach to airstrip and unloading

Initially, we were operating out of the airport at Sentani, on the coast, close to the capitol of Jayapura but then moved the operation to Wamena in a big, high valley in the central mountains. The MAF had Cessna Caravans,

206's, 185's and a Hughes 500 chopper, the Red Cross had a Huey helicopter, the Australian Army had five Blackhawk helicopters, a de Havilland Cariboo, and we with a Twin Otter. MAF had also brought in a Twin Otter but crashed it on the third day of operations but fortunately no one was hurt.

The Aussie troops rotated out every thirty days and a new group came in. They were a little on the wild side just before returning home, drank a lot and ran around the airport dressed only in a penis gourds they had bought from villagers. Of course, with their white butts they looked quite comical compared the dark-skinned Melanesians.

Dressed up for a dignitary's arrival

Where to put the seatbelt?

*Red Cross chopper forwarded food from our plane
into villages without landing strips*

Short people

Occasionally a teenager from Koropun, one of the
outlying villages, who was going to high school in

Wamena would hang around the airport when we were loading and practice his English on us. His English was actually quite good, and he was very interested in the airplane and everything we were doing. He hadn't been home for the two years since he'd been in high school but was planning to go home the next Christmas. We asked how he would get there, and he simply said, "Walk". It was a 25-minute flight and he said it would take him three days to walk home, and three more to walk back. One day we snuck him on the plane and took him to Koropun with us. When we opened the door and he stepped out, he was *King for a Day*. The village went absolutely nuts. We had another load to bring in, so we picked him up a couple hours later. There are no roads to those mountain villages, only rough foot paths.

The Red Cross had determined that rice had the most protein per pound and it was bagged in 50 Kg. (110 lb.) burlap sacks which I also helped unload. Between that physical work and three small Indonesian style meals a day I was getting into the best shape I was in since Army days. Then somebody decided to bag the rice in 100 Kg. sacks and I could almost feel the disks in my vertebrae bursting and wisely quit carrying those 220-pound bags. Those tough, short little Papuans, barefoot and wearing only a penis gourd, would carry those heavy bags a quarter mile across rocks to a shelter. One strip we flew into always brought out all the chickens in the village when they heard our plane because it meant some spilled rice on the ground.

100 kilos (220 pounds)
136

Just an observation: When missionaries began bringing Christianity to the natives of New Guinea and building airstrips in the 1950's, there were some turf wars. It was decided to split up Irian Jaya and give the various denominations exclusive rights to certain areas – Baptist, Seventh Day Adventist, Catholic, Episcopal, etc.

This probably had a practical side too since there are over 300 languages and dialects spoken on the Island. Villages within sight of each other, but on the other side of steep river valleys, would take days to reach each other on foot and probably could not converse verbally. My observation was that the various villages we flew into seemed quite different socially. In some, the women, wore only grass skirts and naked children gathered in one group and the men, wearing only penis gourds in another group. In a different village all of the residents might be somewhat clothed and intermingling, with a woman even ordering men to pick up a sack and put it here or there. My question: Were these villages always so different or was it the influence of different religious groups in their area?

When the rains had returned, one MAF pilot noted the planting should have resumed but hadn't. He asked one villager why they weren't planting, and the reply was that they didn't have to anymore because we brought them food now. *It's easy for people to get dependent but* towards the end of the food lift the natives around the village of Silimo gave us a wonderful send off. Many hundreds showed up outside the village dressed in their Sunday finest and danced, sang, roasted a pig and gave speeches of thanks. What more could one ask for?

Upon returning home the job search began again. The pilot who had replaced me at Aeronautical Services five years prior was still there, but I kept busy doing long neglected work around our house and sending out resumes. One Friday I ran into Jim Wilson in town, who I had surveyed for 24 years prior, and jokingly asked if he needed a surveyor. He said. "Be at the office at eight Monday morning". I told him that I was more or less joking because I was really looking for a flying job, but he said that he understood. That was the third time that he had hired me. Oh, my goodness, had the surveying technology changed in that 24 years. When I quit surveying in 1974 we were basically still doing it the way the Egyptians had 3000-years before, measuring a distance with a tape, turning an angle with some kind of theodolite and calculating positions using basic trigonometry. We did get those newly invented calculators in 1969 which cost $400 then and can be bought in the Dollar Store now.

CHAPTER 13
AIRSERV - HONDURAS

Hurricane Mitch hit Central America in late October 1998 with sustained winds of over 180 mph and heavy rains. It destroyed 75% of the bridges and killed over 7,000 people in Honduras alone. The Mosquito Coast in the southeastern part of the country was completely cut off from any roads. MAF was working with a number of missionary groups there and sent out a plea for help and AirServ responded. They didn't have any planes in the Americas but found that Kenmore Air near Seattle had an extra turbine Otter they would rent out during their slow season. A deal was struck, and they took it off floats and put it on wheels with big tires for us.

The phone rang and it sounded much more interesting than surveying, so I joined Rob Stone, we got checked out, picked up the plane in Seattle and headed for Honduras. Rob was an invaluable copilot. He spoke fluent Spanish and had been stationed there in the Air Force a few years prior and knew his way around. Even though the original 600 horsepower Pratt & Whitney radial engine had been replaced with a 750-horsepower turbine engine, the drag from the big tires and fat wings still made for a slow trip but it was interesting seeing how the topography and vegetation varied from one end of Mexico to the other. As we got into Central America we began seeing the effects of Hurricane Mitch. It was unbelievable! The huge banana plantations were stripped with only the bare trunks remaining. Vegetation was ripped away and brown, bridges destroyed, and rivers filled with debris.

At San Pedro Sula, where we checked in for Customs, the water marks in the airport terminal building were six feet up the walls. As we flew into the airport at Tegucigalpa, the capital, a huge earth slide was visible where many hundreds of houses once stood.

AirServ had arranged for an apartment for us in Tegus (nickname for the capital) but we were to be operating out of Soto Cano, a joint US and Honduran air force base, about forty miles to the north. From there we would load up and make two to three round trips a day to the Mosquito Coast. It was a lot of flying so we were also looking for an airport closer to our destination that still had road transportation to the outside for logistics. We saw one that had possibilities and landed to check it out. As we were shutting down, men in camouflage and armed with M-16's came out of the bush and surrounded us. We got out and asked, "Who are you"? to which they replied, "Who are YOU"? One guy wearing a tee shirt had a US Marines tattoo on his arm which made me feel a little less anxious. They were part of a US DEA drug interdiction team watching for suspicious aircraft activity. It turned out that moving the whole operation would have been more trouble than it was worth, so we kept operating out of Soto Cano. A skinny little African American buck sergeant (E-5), who had been refueling us, mentioned that she had just reached her twenty years in the Air Force and was retiring in three weeks. Unfortunately, the retirement pay for an E-5 wouldn't be very much and I asked her what her retirement plans were. She said, "I'm goin' back up to Georgia and help Jimmy Carter build houses fo' poor folk". Wow! How can you not love and respect somebody like that?

Unloading the turbine Otter

One of the villages we were flying into had two airstrips – one right next to the village and another much better one across a river about four miles away. When we landed at the better one, the Padre at the village said that if we could land next to the village it would save them a lot of valuable gasoline and the danger of crossing the river, so we did, once. The strip was short and covered with mud and two inches of water. We made it but without much room to spare so I made a tough decision. I told the Padre that we could not consistently fly into that marginal strip without risking damage to the plane. If that happened we'd be permanently out of business for the sake of saving some gas. I think he understood.

We had flown a number of loads into the village of Ahuas but when we brought in a load for a neighboring village without a strip, people just stood around and nobody volunteered to help unload the plane. I got out and asked what was going on. Finally, a guy who spoke English came over and said they were mad because this load wasn't for them. I was fuming and told him to tell the group standing around that if they didn't help I'd NEVER come back to Ahuas. Reluctantly they helped.

The MAF man in charge of the operation was a retired Air Force Special Ops guy who didn't have it all together. The whole affair was certainly interesting but in my opinion an ineffective waste of money. There needed to be much better communications between the needy villages and the logistician in charge to see that we weren't taking clothing to people who had clothes and cook ware to people without food. It was a sad way to end my flying with AirServ and I think we would have been much more effective had AirServ been in charge. The flight back up to Seattle was uneventful except for the hassle given to us by a customs man in Villahermosa, Mexico, holding us up for three hours trying to extract a bribe. When I got home, Rica said that Aeronautical Services had just called and was wondering if I was available.

CHAPTER 14
"OTTERS" AGAIN

The last five years had been a great adventure, but it was also great to be home again. Since Rica and I left Loki, the jobs with AirServ had been short term, solo deployments. Being close to friends and family definitely has its pluses. Getting back into the Otters was like putting on an old shoe and other than planning to build our new house not much had changed. Occasionally Mike, our operations manager would meet me after a flight and ask if I'd been playing around again, to which I'd ask if the phones had been ringing again.

Otter delivering UPS freight to a San Juan Island

Since the copilot's seat was usually empty I'd often enlist the help of friends and family to become temporary, unpaid employees to fly along with me to help unload the planes. No shortage of volunteers!

My favorite copilot

Life was good but one day Mike got us together with some somber news. UPS had gotten a new manager who didn't like airplanes. He casually asked Mike what we did with the freight on foggy days and when we couldn't fly. Mike said that we then put the trucks on the ferry. It didn't take UPS long to figure out that that would be much cheaper than flying the freight and the contract that ASI had for 24 years was terminated. My last flight in an Otter was in November 2000.

CHAPTER 15
EMPIRE AIRLINES

I had some severance pay from ASI and with the equity we had in our old house I used my free time to work on our new home – wiring, plumbing, decks, cabinets, etc. In our annual Christmas letter for 2000 I mentioned that I was unemployed again but making good use of my time building our new house. I'd sent one to an old friend, Tim Komberec, from Cascade Airways who was now CEO of Empire Airlines, a large company operating many of the FedEx feeder aircraft in the western US. Damn, I was kinda enjoying this enforced retirement, but Tim offered me a job flying a FedEx Cessna Caravan. It wasn't a jet with international routes and back to first year salaries again, but it was close to home and had insurance, sick leave, vacation, 401K, etc.

My domicile was Seattle, but Empire furnished me with an apartment there and on my days off I'd head home to Lake Samish. There were four Caravans based in Seattle. One went to Port Angeles for the day, the next to Burlington, and the last, which I usually flew, went to Bellingham, Orcas Island and then spent the day in Friday Harbor on San Juan Island. They had a motel room for the pilot to lounge in and then in the evening they'd reverse the route back to Seattle. The fourth

Freight moving from trucks to Caravan and then to the MD-11

plane was a spare for overloads, mechanicals or whatever. My days in Friday Harbor were usually spent reading, walking around the docks looking at sailboats, having lunch with Roy Franklin and other old friends or sleeping. FedEx's whole *modus operandi* was based on "on time" and they took it very seriously. If you were more than two minutes late for departure they required a full-page explanation of why you were late and why it won't happen again. Any hiccup—in the chain of events that moved an envelope from your business or home to the airport during a snow storm, onto a Caravan that needed loading and de-icing, getting a slot in flow control to Seattle during rush hour—was cause for concern because a DC-10 was waiting for you. Every flight was done under instrument flight rules. No more circling a pod of Orcas or submarine, flying along shorelines looking at our awesome scenery. This was so contrary to the kind of flying that I loved that on my 62nd birthday I filed for Social Security.

As I was taxiing into the ramp at SEATAC on May 31, 2002 a voice on the ground control frequency said, "Congratulations, Captain Herrmann". While I was trying to figure out who might have said that, I noticed a couple of fire trucks by our ramp and thought there must be some kind of drill going on. Just as I taxied between them they opened up over my plane in a huge arc from their water cannons and when I shut down, somewhat shaken, the fire chief opened the door and congratulated me on my retirement.

Then my colleagues doused me with champagne and a few days later they and other flying buddies attended my retirement party and appropriately, the hangar flying was knee high to a giraffe. **NEVER FLEW JETS...... but had a lot of fun.**

CHAPTER 16
OUR AIRPLANES

REPUBLIC RC-3 "SEABEE" 1976-1977

July 1954 - I was 13 years old and my mother wanted to visit her ailing mother on the small farm in Bavaria where she grew up. I spoke little German and they spoke no English at all. I found an old English language 1946 *Popular Mechanics* magazine in a pile of old periodicals and saw an article featuring an all metal, four place amphibious airplane. This sounded like the ultimate traveling machine and I said that someday I'd have one. It took 22 years but in November 1976 the whole family joined me on a trip to Midland, Michigan to pick up my dream machine.

The 1947 Seabee had a rather bulbous nose, pusher prop, no heater, an overrated 215 horsepower Franklin engine and the landing gear and flaps were operated by a hydraulic hand pump handle located between the seats. The seats and large windows were ahead of the wings which made for superb visibility and that was great because its leisurely forward speed gave you plenty of time to contemplate the countryside slowly passing below. We had a 30 knot headwind most of the way home to San Juan Island and it didn't take too long before the kids got bored and said, I'm cold or the cars are passing us or I'm hungry or I have to go to the bathroom or when will we get there, etc. As we approached the Mississippi River I thought it might be memorable to shoot a touch 'n go on that great river but the thought of giving up that 4000' of slowly gained altitude squelched the idea. The plane had very little in the way of instruments or navigation gear which made finding our next airport in Fort Dodge, Iowa, in a snowstorm a challenge. We managed and got gas there and then proceeded to Yankton, South Dakota, where the wind was 25 knots straight down the runway. The landing was no problem but, since an airplane is designed pretty much like a giant weathervane, I couldn't get it to turn around to taxi back down the runway to the fuel pit. For some reason the tail wheel steering was ineffective, so I had to use the right and left brakes to steer, which were also somewhat ineffective. When I did get the plane turned around and taxied down wind, a gust would hit and spin the plane back around into the wind. One time I hit the right brake too hard and instead of turning back downwind it stood right up on its nose and then slammed back on the tail wheel again with a huge "thump". I had to get off the runway and my dream machine was turning into an uncooperative monster. After repeated tries and riding the brakes so hard that the brake fluid was boiling out the master cylinders, we made it. The gas boy was also a mechanic, flight instructor and aspiring airline pilot so we immediately hit it off and he said we should push the plane into a nearby hangar where he quickly found the problem; one of the control cables going to the tail wheel steering had come off its pulley. He replaced it and since it was getting late he offered us the use of his car to find a motel and get something to eat.

The next morning it was quite cold, and we had to pre-heat the engine to get it started. Just after takeoff I looked at the airspeed indicator and it was stuck at zero. Now what! Since we were already in the air and I knew we weren't going to break any speed limits we just continued on to our next fuel stop at a little crop duster strip at Chamberlain, South Dakota. Rica and the kids went into the trailer/office to thaw out while I took the pitot system apart and thawed out some water that had frozen in it, then on to Rapid City where we spent the night. The next morning as I was trying to start the plane something in the throttle linkage didn't feel right. Sure enough, the wire in the cable housing leading to the throttle had frozen and when I advanced it while starting the engine the wire had bent. It was Saturday and they had to call in a mechanic. The Seabee is a rare bird, only 1060 built, and ours also had some modifications so naturally they didn't have the parts needed to fix it. Finally, by late evening we had it fixed, and we spent another night in Rapid City. I called work to tell them that we'd be a little late getting back and Rica was beginning to think that this whole idea was bad, bad, bad.

Two days later on our trip, we went to the weather office in Missoula to check Spokane's weather. It didn't look so good and Rica said she just couldn't go any further, grabbed the kids and their bags and caught the next bus to Seattle. I took off and flew to Coeur 'd Alene alone where I checked the weather again and decided to give it a try, figuring that once I got into the flatlands of central Washington it would be okay. I followed Interstate 90 to about twenty miles past Spokane when the clouds just got too low to continue and returned to Spokane. They cleared me to land on Runway 21 and after landing I made a sharp left turn for a taxiway to parking. This may have caused the carburetor float to stick causing the engine to die. I hit the starter and the hot engine just grunted but wouldn't turn over. The tower called and said, "Seabee 63K, expedite off the runway. 737 on short final". I tried to explain that my engine had died but they just repeated the previous command, but in an octave higher voice. I jumped out of the plane and began hand propping the damn Franklin engine just as a Western Airlines 737 had to go around and flew right over the top of us. The engine finally caught, and I jumped back in the plane and requested permission to taxi to parking. The controller said, "Roger, taxi to parking – and get that damn thing fixed". I caught the next bus to Seattle. A few days later the weather cleared, and a friend flew me to Spokane to pick up our bird and fly it home to Friday Harbor.

That winter we dressed warm and enjoyed flying around to lakes and runways in Washington till it was time for the annual inspection. Bad compression on two cylinders meant some engine repairs were necessary. According to the logbooks, the engine had a partial overhaul only 91-hours prior, but the valve guides were already allowing leakage past the valves. I took all the cylinders to an old mechanic in Seattle who had worked on many Seabees in years gone by and he explained that this particular engine wasn't used on any other planes, consequently, since there were relatively few of them around, not much after market development was done for them. The original engine, in 1946, had cast iron valve guides which weren't very durable, and no one had gone through the trouble of certifying a better replacement part. What he used to do is machine down the bronze guides used on Pratt & Whitney radial engines. They worked great but because they weren't certified you couldn't tell anyone who had done the repair. Mum's the word.

By summer I couldn't wait to take our plane on a camping trip. I had a friend with a Cessna 172 on floats and another with a Lake amphibian who were interested in joining us on a three-day trip to Vancouver Island. Two of us cleared customs at the Victoria airport and the floatplane cleared at the seaplane base and we met up again at Shawnigan Lake, about 15-miles west. From there we flew up the rugged west coast of Vancouver Island, graveyard of many hapless ships driven ashore by the strong on shore winds. It was so common that a trail was constructed above the shoreline that survivors of shipwrecks could hike the trail to help. We decided to land at Nitinat Lake, a beautiful spot above the shoreline.

172 and Seabee on the sandy beach
on Cowichan Lake on Vancouver Island

After landing the two amphibs put their wheels down and taxied up on a beach. We got out without even getting our feet wet and helped the floatplane get turned around and backed up on the sandy shore. I walked onto the floats and scooped up a handful of the crystal-clear water for a drink. Yuck - it was salty! There is a lot of saltwater around Puget Sound, but I had carefully avoided landing in it as a precaution against corrosion and rust but unbeknownst to us, Nitinat Lake was low enough that during high tides and storms sea water backed up into the lake. After lunch we flew to a freshwater lake, landed and then put our wheels down and splashed around as much as we could to wash the salt off our planes.

The float plane needed gas, so we then flew to Sprout Lake, which had a seaplane base. As it came into view in the distance it appeared that there were two large structures in the lake, near the east end, maybe hotels or something. No – as we got closer it appeared that they were two huge airplanes.

They were, in fact the largest operational aircraft in existence when built in the 1940's – the Martin Mars flying boat. Six were built for the US Navy and upon retirement were bought by Forest Industries Flying Tankers in Canada and converted to water bombers. We taxied up the nearby ramp and walked around looking for someone to sell us gas. We walked through the shop and it was deserted. Out the other door it was apparent that they were all gathered in and around the Seabee, admiring it like the latest Ferrari at a car show. I should have taken that opportunity to ask them for a tour of **their** seaplane. They operate two of these monsters around western North America during the fire season and used the remaining ones for spare parts.

The Seabee attracted attention wherever it went. One onlooker, viewing the pusher prop in the middle of the fuselage, asked, "Which way does this thing go?" That pusher prop also was reversible, ostensibly to make docking easier but when the engine was hot and the oil, which operated the prop pitch, was thin there wasn't enough oil pressure at idle to move the blades into reverse. This required a real juggling act when approaching a dock because as you got close to the dock you had to add power to raise the oil pressure to move the prop from forward into reverse before you crashed into the dock, or just shut the engine off further from a dock and throw a rope for someone to pull you in. It was fun to pull straight into a gas pump and after fueling watch the onlookers faces as you started the engine and then backed away from the gas pumps. The plane's instrument panel only went half-way across the cockpit so the co-pilot could open the bow door and step right onto the dock and it was also great place to fish from. The seat backs were supposed to fold flat into beds, making it a flying RV. How cool is that? Unfortunately, the latching mechanism on ours didn't work or had been modified so we brought a tent.

Our Seabee cruised between 90 and 105 miles per hour, depending on our weight. It had a modification whereby we could easily take off the landing gear if you were flying from water to water and the reduced drag added 15 MPH to your cruise speed. It was opening day of fishing season and I invited my brother and an uncle to fly to Ross Lake, planning to take the wheels off at my brother's house at Lake Samish. Unfortunately, about this time we had decided to sell the plane and use the money to build a house and advertised it in *Trade-A-Plane*, a trade publication, thinking it would take weeks or months to sell such an odd plane. A guy flew up from California three days later, handed me a check and took my plane. Fishing trip canceled and I had tears in my eyes as we watched him take off and head south with my pride and joy.

My ultimate dream had always been to spend my first summer of retirement with a Seabee in the Alaska back country, but the reality of that dream just didn't mesh with Social Security, the Seabee burning 15 gallons of gas per hour and Rica's fears of sleeping in a tent in grizzly country.

PIPER PA 22/20 "PACER" 1983-1989

At this point I was driving 50 passenger turboprops with pressurization, autopilots and trying not to spill any drinks but I really began to miss *flying.* Pilots are a rather fussy lot and selecting an airplane is a very personal thing with many things to consider: horsepower, engine make, useful load, fuel burn, range, speed, number of seats, metal, fabric, conventional gear, taildragger, retractable, high wing, low wing, fixed pitch prop or controllable, takeoff and landing distances, rough and short field capable, etc. Naturally, the economics of all these choices also weighed heavily into the final decision.

After years of contemplation I decided on a Piper that would fit the bill. Its heritage goes all the way back to the 1937, 40 horsepower Piper J-3 Cub, or even earlier. It had a steel tube fuselage and wooden wings covered with cotton fabric and seated two people in tandem. Over the years it had morphed through many different variants culminating in the PA-22 Tripacer which had 160 horsepower, seated four people and was built up until 1963.

A colleague told me about a plane he'd heard about at a small airport in central Washington that sounded just about right. I called the owner up and arranged to come and look it over. It was a blue and white 1956 Tripacer

160

with a very reliable 150 horsepower Lycoming engine and had been converted from tricycle gear back to a taildragger. The low price of $5500 reflected the fairly high hours on the engine and its lack of radios. SOLD! In a few days Rica drove me back with a check in hand and I flew "Stubby" back to an outlying field where I telephoned the control tower at Walla Walla and told them I was coming in without a radio. As I approached they flashed a green light at me, and I was cleared to land. When our daughter, Liana, came out to the airport after school to look at our new toy she said, "It sure looks stubby" and the name stuck.

Proud owners of our second airplane

Cascade Airways' main maintenance base was at Walla Walla and they let employees buy parts and radios at cost with payroll deductions. I was in hog heaven. We used car gas in the plane which was about half the cost of aviation fuel and went flying at every opportunity. Northern Idaho has some of the best back country airstrips anywhere and we tried to check them all out, pitching our tent right next to Stubby. We were camped next to the Salmon River one time and a river raft pulled ashore and some very excited people came to our camp and asked where the ranger was. As they had come through some rapids upriver they found a deflated raft and a bunch of gear, cameras, tent, sleeping bags, etc., strewn among the rocks but no people. We pointed out the ranger's cabin and they went to report the accident; we volunteered to do an aerial search if he felt it might help. He said thanks and after some investigation determined that the owners of the ruined raft had pulled on to a sandbar for lunch. Unfortunately, they hadn't realized that as the day warmed and more snow melted, the river rose, and their raft floated away without them.

Another time I had invited my brother along for a flight to Fish Lake, to go fishing. It is at 6000' elevation and the short strip begins right at the water's edge and goes up a hillside. The trout were numerous but small, so we enjoyed hiking around and watching the wildlife, especially the mooses (meese?). The day we planned to leave, we got up early to take off in the cool, denser air. As we were picking up speed down the runway a giant bull moose walked into the middle of the strip and stopped to see where the (our) noise was coming from. We were going too fast to stop and too slow to fly and a bloody collision seemed eminent when the creature finally decided to amble off the runway. Whew!

We often flew between Walla Walla and Bellingham to visit family and I never tired of flying over the Cascade Mountains. Sometimes I did feel guilty though as we flew past the awesome, rugged mountain peaks in the comfort of our little, heated plane and observed climbers struggling up the mountains.

One trip Rica fondly remembers was a long weekend in July where we covered a lot of ground in a few days. The plane was loaded and as soon as our daughter Christy got off work on Thursday, we flew to Ranger Creek, an airstrip in the mountains just north of Mount Rainier. We ate a great picnic dinner and then rolled out our sleeping bags and had a wonderful night sleeping under the stars. The next morning, we flew to Crest Airpark in Kent and taxied into Rica's sister's back yard and spent the day visiting her. That evening we flew to Friday Harbor and pitched our tent in the tie down area and walked to the harbor with a sail we had brought from Walla Walla for friends who were sailing in the San Juans. They invited us to go sailing with them the next day. On Sunday we visited some friends who had an airstrip on their property and our daughter caught San Juan Airlines to Seattle and Cascade Airways back to Walla Walla. Monday we flew to Bellingham and spent the day visiting my parents and that evening flew to Stehekin, a small airstrip at the north end of Lake Chelan, in the Cascade

Mountains and pitched our tent again. Tuesday we flew to Kennewick Airport, which is right next to a large mall, did some shopping and then flew home.

A friend, Chuck Grady who also owned a Pacer, told me about a guy he knew who cut a Honda 90 Trail (small motorcycle) in half and then fabricated some parts so it could easily be reassembled again. The idea was that if you took the back seat out of a Pacer, you could put the two halves of the bike in the back and have transportation when you got to another airport. We both already had the Honda 90's and went to work.

A few months later another friend, Howard Strickland who had a grass strip on his dairy farm, called and wondered if I wanted to ride along when he drove to Seattle to get some airplane parts. I said, "Sure, but I've got a better idea. I'll pick you up about ten and we'll take our plane". He wondered how we'd get from Boeing Field to the parts house, but I assured him that I had it covered. I had to chase the cows off his grass landing strip and when I came back around and landed, the fresh "cow pies" made a mess of my plane. Oh well! When we got to Galvin Aviation at Boeing Field they parked us between an immaculate Lear Jet and a beautiful three engine Falcon jet. We jumped out and assembled the Honda on the ramp and both rode away on it. As we were leaving the airport Howard said, "I'll bet those corporate pilots we parked next to are wondering where the hell we came from – a fabric covered taildragger splattered with cow shit and a motorcycle in the back seat?" We probably smelled like a dairy farm too.

Over the eight years that we owned "Stubby," he never let us down and gave us and many friends countless hours of great pleasure, although for the first few years Rica couldn't relax. That really bothered me and one day I said, "If you don't like my flying, you fly" to which

Our Piper PA-22/20 "Pacer" aka "Stubby"

she replied, "I don't know how". "I'll show you. Grab the wheel – push to go down and pull to go up and turn left to go left and right to go right". After a few apprehensive minutes she calmed down a little and realized that it wasn't that hard. Then she asked what those foot pedals were for and I pointed out a little curved glass tube on the instrument panel that had a black marble in it. If the ball is in the center of the tube you are in smooth, coordinated flight and you keep it there with those foot pedals. If the ball is to the right of center you step on the right pedal to bring it back to the middle and vice versa. Then I had her make a series of 90-degree left and right turns all the way back to Walla Walla. I'm sure that an air traffic controller watching us on radar was wondering what the heck we were doing. Suddenly, as if a bright light came on Rica exclaimed, "You have to bank the airplane to make it turn. I thought you did that just to scare me". She never did have a desire to take off or land but did attend a private pilot ground school and became an excellent navigator.

Cascade Airways folded in March, 1986 and there was nothing to keep us in Walla Walla, so the house was put up for sale and the job search began, but suddenly I realized that this break presented an opportunity for a great adventure. This was the time that Mikhail Gorbachev was president of the Soviet Union and pushing "glasnost" or openness and the lessening of the Cold War tensions between our two countries. In that spirit I mentioned to Rica that we could put a big auxiliary fuel tank where the back seat was, and I could fly Stubby to Europe where she could rejoin me for a trip through Europe, Asia, Alaska and home again. She humored me as I wrote the Soviet Embassy asking for permission to fly through their country, knowing full well that we would probably be turned down. "Nyet", but the joker up my sleeve was to write Gorbachev personally and ask, in the spirit of glasnost, for permission to make this trip. At this point Rica felt that I was getting entirely too serious about this trip and also said "nyet". Oh well!

At one point we had to have the engine and prop overhauled and we had installed a new instrument panel with good radios and gyros. Stubby was just the way I wanted it but two employers in a row had gone bankrupt and I ended up hauling freight in a noisy single engine airplane. For relaxation I thought sailing would be preferable to jumping into another small, noisy airplane in my free time, so I put a for sale sign in the window and within two months Stubby had found a new home. Years later, after I'd retired, the desire to fly again and the fun we had with Stubby became so overwhelming that I bought a wrecked Piper Pacer with the thought of rebuilding it. I've had a number of friends who have made home-built planes and figured I could rebuild this one. Well, there is a big difference between a certificated airplane and a home built. All parts, materials, radios, screws and even upholstery on a certificated plane must be FAA approved and costs significantly more than what can be used on a home-built plane and all work must be done or signed off by an appropriately licensed mechanic. This wasn't working out the way I had anticipated, and Rica didn't like sailing, so I sold the sailboat and the Pacer project and got a motorcycle and headed for Mexico.

Made in the USA
Middletown, DE
12 October 2022

12555792R00106